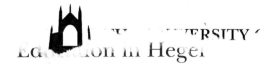

Education in Hegel

D1323637

Also available from Continuum:

Continuum Studies in Educational Research

Philosophy of Education by Richard Pring
Theory of Education by David Turner
Hegel's Philosophy of Right by David James

Education in Hegel

Nigel Tubbs

continuum

Continuum International Publishing Group

The Tower Building
11 York Road
London SE1 7NX

80 Maiden Lane
Suite 704
New York NY 10038

www.continuumbooks.com

British Library Cataloguing-in-Publication Data
A catalogue record for this book is available from the British Library.

ISBN: 978-1-4411-9227-1 (papercover)

Library of Congress Cataloging-in-Publication Data

Tubbs, Nigel.
Education in Hegel / Nigel Tubbs.
   p. cm. – (Continuum studies in educational research)
Includes bibliographical references and index.
ISBN 978-1-4411-9227-1 (papercover)
1. Hegel, Georg Wilhelm Friedrich, 1770-1831. 2. Education–Philosophy.
I. Title. II. Series.

B2948.T83 2008
193–dc22

2008017837

Typeset by Newgen Imaging Systems (P) Ltd, Chennai, India
Printed and bound in Great Britain by MPG Ltd, Cornwall

Contents

Acknowledgements

I thank the University of Winchester, and Anne Williams in particular, for allowing me time to write this book and to research another, and to my colleagues on the Education Studies degree programme – Derek, Simon, Marie, Steph, Wayne and Janice – who have absorbed the consequences of my absence. I also thank Taylor and Francis, and the editors of the Journal *Parallax* for permission to publish an extended version of 'Fossil Fuel Culture', which first appeared in their Journal in 2005, Vol. 11, issue 4, 104–115. The Journal's website can be found at http://www.informaworld. com.

I should like to thank Anthony Haynes for his generous time in commenting on the text. He has improved it considerably while, of course, its weaknesses remain my own. Thanks, too, to Denise Hamilton-Cousins and Hazel Spriggs whose skills kept my pain levels under control; to Dinah Ashcroft whose work with me helps to interrupt the cycle of withdrawal; to Josh who still nourishes from afar; to Marie Morgan and Becky Howes who share the load; and to Julie and Will for being part of my life and for letting me be part of theirs.

My special thanks go to Howard. He has followed me as a benevolent shadow through my work as a teacher and a writer, one characterised by a graceful rigour. He has attended some of my most public moments of greatest intellectual ambivalence, and where others with less consciousness of judgement-power would likely have found little or nothing, he retrieved meaning in the education I work for. Thank you Howie.

Finally, I dedicate this book to Gillian.

Introduction

There can be no learning of learning.

(*Aristotle*, Metaphysics, *XI, 12. 1068b 14*)

I have found that philosophers' relation to education is a strange one. When pressed as to what the point of philosophy is, they may well include education in their answer. However, it is instructive how often this is accompanied by some embarrassment at having very little to say about what exactly this education is and does. One view might, for example, have it that reason in philosophy, employed logically, will overcome false and unjustifiable claims. Philosophical education here is an education through reason to objective epistemological truths and moral values. Another view might see education in philosophy as a form of critique regarding the ways in which reason is employed to serve vested political and philosophical interests and dogmas. Nietzsche, for one, argues that metaphysics, theology, psychology and epistemology have all been 'the history of an error' (1982: 485)[1] grounded in the decadence of reason (and the satisfaction of a good meal!).

But whichever philosophical camp is making its claims in this regard, another question is raised. What sort of education is being presupposed in any philosophizing that bids us to read it and to learn from it? What view of education is it that underpins the credentials of philosophical practice, including, or especially, that practice which holds itself educational for us? If no answer is forthcoming here, then the practice is empty of significance. If the answer involves presupposing the kind of thinking which it claims to be proving, then the practice is blind to its own contingency in positing. Either way, and in response to the question of education in philosophy, it is likely that the philosophy of education – or, better, the view of philosophy *as* education – that is at work remains *implied* rather than *explained* by the practitioners. Terms such as 'transform', 'change', 'alter' and 'overcome' when used to justify the effect of philosophy, tend only to erase the philosophical difficulty they represent. It is commonplace for this difficulty to be treated as the least problematic part of a philosophical argument. In fact, it is inescapably the ground upon which philosophy is justified as worthwhile

and as having any significance at all. In contrast, then, to the nervousness
that avoids explaining how philosophy is educational and what this might
mean for the identity and significance of philosophy, it will be part of the
argument presented in *Education in Hegel* that what makes Hegel's philosophy so profoundly difficult and rewarding is that it works in the full
awareness of having education as its own essence, that is, as the very substance of what it is and does. I will be presenting this education as formed
within and formative of the relations of life and death and master and slave,
as known to itself in and as recollection and as having its truth in the notion
of the *Aufhebung*. In turn, I will argue that it is within this education that the
absolute in Hegel's philosophy is constituted.

Truth

Even these opening paragraphs, however, bring into play one of the most
controversial claims in Hegel – that the absolute can be thought – as well
as a term that appears to arouse rather less controversy, that of recollection.
I will say something on both of these by way of introduction, for both are
essential to the argument presented in *Education in Hegel*.

To many contemporary commentators in both philosophy and in education, and through them to their students, Hegel has come to symbolize all
that is rotten in the state of modern philosophy. At face value – and only at
face value – for Hegel to claim that he knows the truth is at best ludicrous
and at worst representative of the most inexcusable excesses of Western
arrogance. A popular caricature of Hegel, then, is that he is the archetypal
dead, white, rational, imperialist, male philosopher, perhaps even above all
others. At its height this view of Hegel sees him peddling the kinds of certainties and dogmas in Western philosophical knowledge that give oxygen
to the fire of anti-democratic tendencies of all kinds. His is the philosophy
that must engorge everything that is other to its own way of thinking. It is a
philosophy, as Levinas would say, that in its absolutist pretensions is allergic
to all otherness.

One can respond to such a caricature in different ways and on many
different levels. My response, at least within the scope of this *Introduction*,
is twofold. First, as I intend to demonstrate, education in Hegel works with
a different understanding of what truth is than is common in Western philosophy or, indeed, than the view of truth held within common sense. The
former might hold truth to be that which is in-itself, or an independent
substance or essence. The latter might expect truth to resolve difficult issues
and answer the most intractable human questions. But the absolute in Hegel
is not substance as merely in-itself. Truth in Hegel is subjective substance.

Famously, in the *Introduction* to the *Phenomenology of Spirit*, Hegel sets out in Paragraph 86 how the absolute is to be learned in experience. He notes two experiences: one of an object for a consciousness, and one of the experience of that experience. Since in both cases what is known is mediated in being known, both objects are negated, for each of them is not known in-itself. This is, therefore, a double negation. Thought provides a special case here because what is experienced negatively is the same thing that is doing the negating. As such, this has absolute significance because, even though consciousness only knows itself negatively as what is negated and negating, it knows *itself*. In a moment I will return to this process as one of recollection.

This paragraph in the *Phenomenology* is not intended to be merely an assertion about what truth is. Rather, it is intended that the *Phenomenology* itself will go on to demonstrate it. But it comes across as an assertion, as so much in Hegel does. Why it comes across as an assertion is, however, itself instructive. In any double negation there is the additional significance of its being educative and formative for the mind involved. Education is the third partner here, for education is the name of what is happening. It is when this education is suppressed or masked, or avoided, that Hegelian propositions about truth, as about so many other things, are reduced merely to the status of assertion.

Clearly, a notion of truth grounded in such a negative education is unlike that which one might reasonably expect truth to look like, and certainly different from that which is presupposed in what is referred to as 'formal' philosophy. This is because the absolute in Hegel refers not just to truth that results *from* learning, but also to the truth of itself *as* learning, that is, that the absolute understands the significance for it of negative experiences and comprehends this education to be what truth *is*. It is the purpose of *Education in Hegel* to illustrate below in different ways what this negative knowing, this education, looks like to the modern rational mind as it learns of its own truth from within its own negations. We will see that this truth is an education that comprehends its practice, practises its comprehension, and knows itself to be the whole that, in being true to itself, can only sustain itself as learning.

However, if truth in Hegel is somehow grounded in subjective experience surely this should immediately worry us, for it seems to bring together two things that are incompatible – truth and subjectivity. Should this combination not mean rather the opposite, that truth can *never* be known in-itself and therefore never fully or properly comprehended? But for Hegel this is the whole point. It is not our business to predict what truth should or shouldn't be. We are invited to remain open to learning about truth as we learn about everything else, that is, from experience. That truth is *not* in substance in-itself, because of our subjective experience of it, is the ground or, better, the groundlessness, on which Hegel's absolute is to be found. Truth forms and re-forms itself in what is learned in such difficulties.

Unrest

Second, and still in response to the caricature mentioned above, this in turn gives rise to a tempering of the nature of the absolute in Hegel. At a time, rightly, when there is great caution surrounding notions of truth that appear in the Western philosophical tradition, *Education in Hegel* shows that the absolute in Hegel is not arrogant, although neither is it timid. Rather, as with the project of *Education in Hegel* overall, the absolute is modest in the weakness that characterizes it and immodest in presenting this weakness. This is a spiritual and philosophical notion of truth. It is not, again, truth as a standpoint or a dogma, yet crucially it does retain standpoint and dogma within its own conception of truth. There is no more rigorous critique of the whole basis of a standpoint in modern Western thinking than Hegel.[2] What makes Hegel's critique of standpoint so compelling is that it never avoids the ways in which a critique of standpoint opposes itself and, in addition, it never presupposes the meaning of this self-opposition outside of the education that it performs. As such, Hegel is able to offer both a critique of bourgeois rational mastery and at the same time a philosophical and political critique of the complicity of that critique in what it opposes. This means that education in Hegel is not a formal intellectual exercise, it is the work of the *actual* intellect, and it is within the nature of actuality that an immanent critique of standpoint leaves itself groundless. This, I will argue, is exactly the nature of education in Hegel. It is the truth of the groundlessness of all standpoints. Indeed, the integrity of Hegelian thinking is that it does not avoid its own abstraction in standpoint. Education in Hegel retains all its own misrecognitions but comes to know them differently.

In addition, here, we should note that it is in the nature of education not to rest with itself. The difficulty but also the power of Hegelian philosophy is that truth in Hegel is compelled to re-learn about itself, from itself, in whatever situation it faces. It cannot rest, because education is the truth of unrest. To borrow an expression from Derrida, further explored in Chapter 4, education and learning have the unrest of autoimmunity as their own truth.

In passing, we should note also that this integrity of non-avoidance of unrest in what is being negated calls for a rigour that has less to do with the scholastic and more, much more, to do with the pursuit of the truth of the negations in one's life. The rigour of such education in Hegel lies in the risk of its unrest and in the struggle for the meaning of this unrest in human relations. This integrity, the integrity of learning that will not stop with itself, begins with Socrates in Ancient Athens. In Hegel the annoying gadfly of philosophical questioning learns more about its truth than Socrates could have done. But it lives on. Philosophy is not at an end in Hegel. It is in the throes of another period of development, of its own re-formation. *Education in Hegel* aims to contribute to our understanding of this modern education and development. This is why the book is written as it is. It does not pursue education in Hegel through a scholarly exegesis of the concept of education in all his work. Nor does it undertake an historical survey as to when and how Hegel's philosophy has been employed as educational method within institutional education. I have no doubt that this alone will not recommend the book to many who work closely with Hegel. Instead, I have taken from Hegel what I consider to be his most central and his most illuminating insight into philosophy – that it has its truth as education – and brought it out of his texts to speak where possible to twenty-first century issues and problems. *Education in Hegel* marks only the tip of this deep iceberg, and more remains to be done here than I am even close to being aware of. Nevertheless, I felt it justified to shake the dust off the old man (as Hegel was called as a young man) and to let his educational philosophy emerge in and through the aporetic experiences of some of the most important prejudices that characterize the modern and post-modern world.[3] As such, I have tried to show what we can learn from Hegel about the ways in which we think about inequalities of wealth and power, about freedom and tyranny, and about climate change, as well as about the relation of self and other and of life and death.

As will be seen from the chapters that follow, education in Hegel emphasizes meaning rather than solution, and this again may frustrate those readers who want not merely to interpret the world but to know how to change it. I hope that, in what follows, education in Hegel might begin to persuade them of the need also to comprehend the actuality of their desire.

Mutuality

I feel it pertinent in this *Introduction* to mark out two standpoints in particular that education in Hegel opposes. The first of these is mutual recognition. It is a central tenet of *Education in Hegel* that his contribution to the idea of the social, political and global 'other' lays elsewhere than in mutual recognition. The latter posits a middle between individuals that cannot be thought by a self-consciousness in modern social and political relations. Mutuality is present only aporetically in its autoimmunity to itself. It is, as such, a spiritual event. As we will see in Chapter 1, the life and death struggle in Hegel's *Phenomenology of Spirit* is not the effect of a political struggle for recognition, it is the origin of the political *per se* and is masked as this origin precisely by that which it produces, namely, the political. The second standpoint is that of post-foundational philosophy, taken here with a broad brush – but not so in Chapters 4 and 5 – which posits a mutuality of difference. The claim for a radical heterogeneity between self and other, between cultures, and between subjectivity and the absolutely other, is itself underpinned by a middle of mutuality in which all are the same in being different. Mutual recognition of the same, and recognition of mutual difference, are two sides of the same coin, whose currency in both cases is an imperialism of the middle, one that is more-or-less – mostly less – acknowledged by its practitioners. Education in Hegel is a critique of such imperialisms, one that refuses for itself a posited grounding in such mutualities while at the same time recognizing its own positing within them.

Life and death

One of the premises in *Education in Hegel*, then, is that modern consciousness is not well educated regarding the relations that it expresses, or about the relations that are present in how consciousness understands itself in the world around it. The most important of these is that despite all of the ways in which it feels sovereign and independent in life, the modern individual is never free from its absolute master, never free from its relation to negation, that is, to death. The free individual is negated by his fear of death, and this fear and negation is what he most fears. But for education in Hegel this negation is formative of modern life. It is an education about death in life, an education that re-forms the truth of the free person.

It might seem strange, even counter-intuitive, for education in Hegel to be arguing for the experience of fear within modern freedom. Is it not patently obvious, a critic might say, to associate fear with regimes that suppress freedom, whether militarily or ideologically, or both? However, in the way that I read Hegel, fear is always a constituent of social and political life, although present in very different ways. What determines political life is how fear, vulnerability and negation are employed, that is, either for security *against* others or for education *about* others. The dictator wields fear as a weapon over those in his dominion because he fears for his own security. Here fear is openly opposed to free self-determination. The market economy, on the other hand, wields freedom as a weapon over its poorer constituents because the consumer fears any negation of its own freedom. Here, the fear of the vulnerability of the free consumer is avoided and made invisible by being exported to others.

Education in Hegel is not arguing here for fear over and against freedom or security or peace of mind; nor, because one fears fear, can it argue against it. Freedom and fear co-exist in ways that shape personal, social, national and global relations. *Education in Hegel* seeks better to comprehend how this is so. It commends freedom to learn from fear – a suppressed people demands freedom from fear which is externally imposed – but also for fear to learn from freedom – a free people can learn of the ambivalence of their freedom when fear, vulnerability and negation are recognized within it.[4] The former will find strength in vulnerability; the latter will find vulnerability in strength. It is the case that, while freedom includes the freedom to learn of fear from within itself, it eschews this education when it forces others to experience fear on its own behalf. This latter is a failure of educational nerve, a failure of freedom to risk its own learning. Fear is what motivates the struggle for freedom, but a freedom that forgets its roots in fear and holds itself (wrongly) to be free from fear, will never be able to learn of others from within itself. This education, in particular, is explored in Chapter 1.

This forms the core of education in Hegel as I will be presenting it. Anticipating the arguments made below for a moment, education in Hegel begins where life learns of its misrecognition of its relation to death. Most importantly, it learns here that the relation of life and death is the template for the social relation of self and other. It learns too, that politics always carries the relation of life and death but in different ways at different times in different historical epochs. Modernity is characterized here by the illusion that life is not of death. This illusion has its cost, its impact, in social and political relations. It is the illusion, for example, that grounds the appearance of bourgeois property law as a natural law between persons, as it does between thought and its relation to its object. This forms the basis of the critique that education in Hegel is able to offer regarding relations between self and other, rich and poor, master and slave, and West and East. I say something on each of these relations in the course of the book. For education in Hegel, then, where life learns of itself as already presupposing a particular relation to death, this is our philosophical education about the spirit of the age. It is also an inclusive and participatory education precisely because it is within the experience of the universality of life and death. Mediaeval philosophers and theologians went to great lengths to protect the masses from speculative truths. Education in Hegel seeks the opposite; not to protect any modern consciousness from its education regarding its own end. It is hard, is it not, to live constantly in relation to negation, to death? Nevertheless education in Hegel teaches that this is the most fundamental relation in human existence. It teaches also, and this is one of its most challenging aspects, that how a human society or culture avoids its relation to death is also the shape of its social and political relations. Or, perhaps more accurately, social and political relations are the actuality of the ways in which life misrecognizes its relation to death.

I can anticipate here the revenge practised against Hegel by a certain kind of supporter of Nietzsche. These supporters might bemoan the way that such talk seems again to be grounded in the spirit of *ressentiment* against life, and to articulate, again, all the hatred of being alive as a human being. In addition, they might abhor the way that fear seems to return here as a value, as a life-denying principle that causes man to be petrified, and then to turn him against himself as if his being alive was the error itself. But I think Nietzsche would not be so vengeful here at the kind of negation at work. Death in education in Hegel is life-affirming; it is in their relation to each other that life seeks itself, and does so against those shapes of itself in thought that seduce it into its own seemingly rational mastery. Did Nietzsche not seek the redemption of man from the error of rationalization viewed as immune from the forces of life and death? And did Zarathustra not respect the tightrope-walker precisely because he lived his life with fear and death against this error?[5] In *Twilight of the Idols*, he says that 'the most spiritual human beings, if we assume they are the most courageous, also experience by far the most painful tragedies: but just for that reason they honour life because it pits its greatest opposition against them' (1982: 524). When life seeks itself in relation to death, this is as much education in Hegel as it is in Nietzsche.[6]

Recollection

The relation of life and death in social relations is educational in and as *recollection*. A few years ago at a seminar in Goldsmith's College, London, I heard the presenter say that the trouble for Hegel in Hegelian philosophy is that 'nothing happens'. This is a wonderful observation but not for the reasons that the presenter intended. He meant to imply that Hegel's philosophy is essentially a tragic and idle tautology. In fact, the phrase 'nothing happens' turns out to be a most pithy yet comprehensive description of Hegelian philosophy and of education in Hegel in particular. Knowing nothing is where nothing *happens*, and this knowing of nothing as *something* is the template of education in Hegel, as indeed it is of the history of Western philosophy in general. The *Aufhebung* is the actuality of this knowing; its substance is its double negation; its subjectivity is the double negation as recollection; and recollection is the education that knows truth in and as the *Aufhebung*. The whole is the way that death, or nothing, or the negative in life, is known by itself.[7] *Spirit, actuality* and the *concept* or the *notion* in Hegel have this *Aufhebung* or this education as their own self-determination.[8]

This notion of recollection that I am arguing for as education in Hegel is differentiated from that in which memory overcomes forgetfulness, as, for example, in the Platonic recollection of separate forms by a corporeal intellect that has forgotten them,[9] or where recollection in Hegel is confined to remembrance.[10] *Education in Hegel* will argue that recollection in Hegel has speculative significance deep within the remembrance of things forgotten. It is because recollection can only recollect itself, that is, can only be in-itself when it is lost as in-itself to the for-itself, that it cannot only be remembrance. Recollection is the remembering of forgetting and the forgetting of remembering known together as educational and philosophical experience. This is how it plays out the speculative and educational significance of Paragraph 86 of the *Phenomenology* referred to above. Recollection recalls its aporetic structure aporetically, and is known to itself in the educational self-(re-)formative structure of the *Aufhebung*, in which what is known is not 'overcome' in its being known. The paradox of this circle that completes itself in its non-completion is the negation of the negation known to itself in the instability and groundlessness that is learning. In fact, it is able to combine the subjectivity of recollection as inwardizing (*Erinnerung*) with the substance of the *Aufhebung* in the actuality of formative experience. The point here is not only that, famously from Hegel's *Philosophy of Right*, the owl of Minerva flies at dusk in recollection of the day's events, that is, as the actual thought of the day which negates events in retrieving them. It is also the case that the owl, or wisdom, knows to risk losing itself in flying again, in that it will be changed by what it learns. Recollection as its own truth is not restricted to the hind-sight of a critical or reflective mind. Rather, the owl of Minerva learns too that only in the groundlessness of the present is the future truly open.[11] This is the educable wisdom of *I-philosophy*[12] that knows to recollect recollection, and knows this as the negative learning of what is negative.

We should not pass over another intriguing aspect of this learning. It is not just death that is able to be known in life in recollection. It is also true for other ideas that are impossible for us, for example, those of infinity, eternity, absolute truth, the nature of God and the origin and purpose of the universe. It is commonplace that the finite human mind cannot grasp the infinite and the eternal. But the nature of their separation is already illusory. As we mentioned above, having them as an object of thought masks the ways in which this relation is already a political shape, a political pre-determination of the relation of thought to the eternal. As life is really death in life, so the finite is really the eternal in life.[13] Recollecting this relation is also part of education in Hegel, just as is recollecting the other in the self, and truth in error. The recollection of these relations is what Hegel means by the education carried in the negation of the negation. It is what happens when negation learns of itself *as learning*.

Let me make this point somewhat differently. When I stare at the stars – and the stars have a noble status in the beginning as in the development of Western philosophy. For example, in the *Metaphysics* Aristotle says that man first philosophized owing to his wonder about the greater matters such as 'the moon and those of the sun and the stars, and about the genesis of the universe' (1984: I. 2. 1982b 12–17) – when I stare at the stars everything changes for me. I lose myself to the vastness of the universe. But I also lose the stars and the universe for they are not what I can see of them. There are two negations here. I am negated by the universe which is itself negated by me, that is, by that which it negates. This is not mutual recognition, nor absolute alterity. It is an education wherein lies the truth of the negation of the negation, a truth that we will come to know in *Education in Hegel* as the social relation wherein 'I am already other and the other is not me'. This can only have substance and subjectivity as education, because it is only as education that something can learn about itself, lose itself in doing so, and remain other than itself even in knowing about itself. This is not esoteric; it is rational, for the truth of reason as education in Hegel is both true and groundless. Openness to this impossibility as learning is the fundamental openness and non-dogmatic character of education in Hegel.

Finally, I have to admit that a book such as this will appear strange to many within the context of present Hegelian commentary. Its argument for the absolute in Hegel will appear anachronistic, and its choice of education as its focus in Hegel is very rare. I am reminded here of Theodor Adorno who said in this regard, 'anyone who is defending something that the spirit of an age rejects as out of date and obsolete is in an awkward position. The arguments put forward sound lame and overdone. He addresses his audience as though he is trying to talk them into buying something they don't want. This drawback has to be reckoned with by those who are not to be dissuaded from philosophy' (1991: 20). Far from being dissuaded, I am resolved to describe here philosophy in Hegel as I have come to know it. I believe the truth of Hegel to lie in education and in learning. I have also found that this truth is never more powerful or more poignant than when it speaks directly to dilemmas and difficulties in life. It speaks to them of the meaning they carry as difficulties and dilemmas, but it does not resolve them, nor do I seek their resolution above all else, as I once did. I don't either seek the tranquillity of mind so aspired to by ancient and mediaeval philosophy. Education in Hegel has its own character, something that speaks of vulnerability and mastery, or of the vulnerable master who remains master and has this remaining master as part of his vulnerability. This approaches the character of the divine in modern life. Perhaps for this reason I have always found education in Hegel more open to teaching than to writing. In previous books I have referred to this education as the contradiction of enlightenment, as philosophy's higher education, and most recently as the philosophy of the teacher. I have also written about how this notion of education has been the substance of an undergraduate programme of studies. I have in this present book not repeated any previously published material on Hegel as a teacher or on some of his more pedagogically inspired texts and letters. But I am also painfully aware that the books fall short of the teaching. Perhaps it is right that this be so. If this book, and the earlier ones, is to be read in the spirit of education that this and they try to capture, then this is less likely to be the case for those who study Hegel among the cobwebs that, he himself warned, stand at the gates of entry to philosophy. It is more likely if it finds readers who experience the unavoidability of the eternal return of perplexity and who, nevertheless, refuse consolation in half-hearted assertions made with a bad conscience. To such readers I have tried to offer a Hegel who speaks to some of the most personal aspects of our experiences of the world and those within it.

The chapters can be read independently of each other, and therefore some repetition of certain key points and ideas has proved unavoidable.[14] Chapter 1 lays out the structure of Hegel's philosophy of the other, and of life and death as they are carried in and by education in Hegel; Chapter 2 finds education in Hegel in the history of philosophy and carries a discussion of different types of education in Hegel, including *Aufhebung* as recollection; Chapter 3 re-thinks fossil fuel culture as a form of modern misrecognition of freedom and brings to bear the substance that pertains to the concept of illusion (*Schein*); Chapters 4 and 5 accept the challenge of relating education in Hegel to Derrida and Levinas respectively; and Chapter 6 experiments with a reading of the *Phenomenology of Spirit* as a modern, reflective, personal and social education.

Notes

1 From *Twilight of the Idols*.
2 I will try to substantiate this claim against Derrida and Levinas in Chapters 4 and 5.
3 Rightly in my view, Donald Verene states that 'so much interpretation of Hegel will not dare anything; it engages [only] in a kind of deft furniture moving' (Verene, 1985: 21).
4 I am reminded here of Nietzsche who, in *Twilight of the Idols*, notes that freedom decays when the struggle for it is deemed complete or institutionalized.
5 This refers to the *Prologue* of Nietzsche's *Thus Spake Zarathustra* (Nietzsche, 1982).
6 There are many other ways in which education in Nietzsche and Hegel could be compared favourably with each other. I have attempted such a comparison in Tubbs, 2005, chapter 7. In a future work tracing the history of Western philosophy I will read Nietzsche and Hegel together as the truth of modernity.
7 This is not a Romantic view of death. It does not mean to infer a recollection that seeks death rather than life. The truth of recollection, rather, is the struggle to know death while alive, and not instead of life.
8 I do not explore the *notion* or the *concept* in the book specifically (although education in Hegel is *das Begriff*), but *actuality* and *spirit* are both discussed in some detail. Also, I have not used capital letters for these and other specialist Hegelian terms, although I have retained them in quotations from translations that do.
9 See, for example, Socrates working with the slave boy in the *Meno* (1956).
10 As, for example, in a recent piece by George Lucas Jr.; see Gallagher, 1997, 97–115.
11 There is another theme in recollection here, that of time. I have not included discussion of this in the present volume, even in regard to the history of philosophy in Chapter 2 (although it does appear towards the end of Chapters 2, 5 and 6). It is something I will return to in a forthcoming history of philosophy as the concept of *future* history of philosophy and its relation as world-spirit. However, in brief, we could say here that the owl of Minerva flies at dusk not just in seeing what this day has taught it, but knowing also that past flying and future flying are both the groundlessness – the learning – of this flight. This is the same wisdom, put more prosaically, that comprehends that just as 'the good old days' are the perspective of present recollection, so, too, present recollection is already 'the good old days' of future recollection. Nietzsche and Kierkegaard both observed that recollection works forwards as well as backwards. As we will see in Chapter 6, this is the actuality of the old man, not old in terms of chronology but in terms of the wisdom of education that knows the past and the future in the present, and knows therein the eternal.

[12] This is the title of Chapter 6.

[13] These are themes I intend to take up again in a forthcoming *History of Philosophy.*

[14] As is the fact that some concepts employed in one chapter might be more fully discussed in another. The most important example of this I think is that recollection, used throughout the work, has its most detailed exposition in Chapter 2.

Chapter 1

Self and Other: Life and Death

Man is born handed over to the necessity of death.

(*Aquinas, 1975b: 212*)

Introduction

In what ways might one be said to learn from the sadness of a funeral? Is it in the way a funeral is a teacher of death in life? Is it because it commends a deep recognition of the truth of death in life? Death is the great universal; we know this. Yet often it takes a funeral, or something of this nature, to bring us to the reminder of where death lies in life. We are of death yet we live as if death is other than life. In fact, life draws a veil over death. Sometimes we see both the veil and its secret. Most times the veil itself is hidden, and in a very particular fashion that will be described below. Either way, education in Hegel teaches us that a philosophy of the other is carried in and by this veil.

In this chapter, then, I want to make the case for a philosophy of the other in Hegel which has its substance in the relation of life and death and in the ways this relation appears as social and political actuality, including that of world spirit. I will try to show how education in Hegel teaches of this relation of death in life as the template for the relations of self and other. In modernity, this relation has form and content in reflective subjectivity but the relation of life and death that determines it is hidden in the illusion of appearing not to be hidden. This is the veil of modern social relations, a transparent freedom that uses its transparency to hide itself. It is seen through but is not itself seen through at all. This is the ambivalent sense in which 'transparent' will be used in this chapter. Hegel's philosophy of the other is an education about the seeming ingenuousness of this (hidden) veil. But we must note even at this early stage, revealing the veil does not mean removing it, for *illusion* is the truth of self and other in Hegel.

Triadic loss

Derrida and Levinas have created the appearance respectively that Hegel cannot accommodate a notion of philosophy that is open to difference or to otherwise-than-being. These claims are explored in Chapters 4 and 5 below. Some who are more sympathetic to Hegel try to claim for him a theory of the other in the model of mutual recognition that is found in paragraphs 178–184 of the *Phenomenology of Spirit*. This, however, is also misleading. It is all too easy to read these paragraphs independently of the part they are playing in the master and slave relation. In fact, mutual recognition in Hegel is written from a standpoint of its being an impossible beginning and end for the self-consciousness that thinks it. Mutual recognition is always already the misrecognition of its being thought. This is the significance of illusion in Hegel, that thought hides its presuppositions behind the freedoms they make possible.

It is from within this misrecognition that Hegel's philosophy of the other is to be found. This means comprehending that his philosophy of the other is a triadic philosophy that concerns not only self and other but also the comprehension of the third partner in their relationship, a third partner who is hidden within the relation of self to other that it determines. This third is pursued in different ways in each of the chapters of this book, but in this chapter it is explored in a very specific way as the hidden third partner in the relation of self and other in Hegel. This requires us to explore, in turn, the determination of the self in loss, the export of loss beyond the self, the hiding of both this loss and its export, and the formative significance of its return. Because the loss and its export are both hidden there can be no simple political unification of self and other, for both are already determined in the deceit, and neither can free itself from its complicity within this appearance of separation. There is, then, a third partner to the self and its other, namely, the aporia that haunts the relation of their being separated. To coin a phrase from Adorno, self and other are torn halves of an integral freedom to which, however, they do not add up. But their dilemma is our education about the incompletion of this relation. Taken as evidence only of failure, and not also of formative political experience, the self can grant itself the right to wallow in the aesthetic of resignation and mourning, and its concomitant, the demand for action. It presumes to know what is wrong with society and what it needs to put it right. But both resignation and the demand for action repeat the truth of the third partner, that is, the failure that accompanies them. There is here a dialectic of enlightenment where resignation calls for action and action returns to resignation. Taken as a whole, this dialectic of enlightenment is the loss of both resignation and the demand for action. What, then, is left? This question and its despair leave us open, now, to begin to explore and to learn the meaning of the self that is loss without ground. I will argue that loss without ground is carried in the ambiguities of the following statement of identity and non-identity: I am already other and the other is not me. In particular, this statement recognizes the complicity of the veiled self even in the statement about its complicity. Loss without ground is the illusion of the self and of its other. But in modern bourgeois social relations, as we will see, even the illusion itself is present as a transparent veil that, as such, cannot be seen. We will, however, begin our study of self and other with a veil that is not veiled, in order to bring out more clearly the nature of the self that it reveals.

The veil

We begin, then, by looking at a short story written by Nathaniel Hawthorne (1804–1864) called 'The Minister's Black Veil'.[1] In this parable the Reverend Mr. Hooper one day appears before his congregation wearing a black crepe veil that drops down over his face. This causes consternation, of a sort that we will explore in a moment, amongst all who know him, including his wife, and to all who subsequently meet him. He never explains the veil, nor does he ever remove it, not even on his own death-bed. He is buried still wearing the veil, but not before he has forced himself, just prior to death, and with a mighty effort, to look around the room at those who are gathered and to announce 'I look around me, and lo! on every visage a Black Veil' (1987: 107). This is a major theme in the short story. When his congregation see the veil, it is as if their Minister has climbed inside them and revealed their darkest thoughts and sins. They hear Hooper preach, through the veil, that they should be prepared for the dreadful hour which will snatch the veil from their own faces.

If this was the sole meaning of the parable – that we all hide behind a veil of some kind; indeed, that it is the truth of the bourgeois to do so – then it would be a wonderfully dramatized critique of *amour-propre* and its intrigues. It would be no less an essay if Hawthorne had confined himself to making this point. We will return to this notion of bourgeois semblance in a moment. However, it is to a different but related aspect of the story that we now turn.

When Hawthorne describes the effect that the veil has on both its audience and its beholder, it is always in the darkest forces of terror and, significantly, of death. I will cite a few examples here. When Hooper attends the funeral of a young girl it is felt that the veil is suddenly not out of place, but rather that it is quite appropriate. Indeed, when Hooper leans over the girl his face would have been visible to her, and one of those assembled there swears that at this moment 'the corpse had slightly shuddered' (1987: 100) as if death had recognized itself in Hooper. Moreover, it is said that it is as if the spirit of the Minister and of the deceased 'were walking hand in hand' (1987: 100). At a wedding the veil inspires in the bride a 'death-like paleness' (1987: 101). Accompanying this partnership of the veil and death are feelings of horror, dread and sorrow which induce, in turn, fear and trembling. Those who are on their own death-beds are indeed drawn to Hooper and they refuse to die until he has come to them. The gloom of the veil 'enabled him to sympathize with all dark affections' (1987: 104). What disturbs Hooper the most is his wife, who leaves him, refusing to have the veil come between them, and the children of the parish who show an 'instinctive dread' (1987: 104) of the veil and flee from Hooper whenever he approaches them.

The veil, then, covers Hooper's face. But, of course, it reveals far more than ever it conceals. It is taken as a sign that Hooper is hiding a secret sin, yet it reveals to those who see it in this way that they are doing the same; such secrets, as they say, that 'we hide from our nearest and dearest, and would feign conceal from our own consciousness, even forgetting that the Omniscient can detect them' (1987: 99). The veil hides Hooper's face from being seen but is interpreted as a turn inwards to reveal his own darkest corners to himself. I wonder, says one lady, that he is not afraid to be so alone with himself. This underestimates just how painful the revelations of the veil are to Hooper. He says to his wife, 'you know not how lonely I am, and how frightened, to be alone behind my black veil' (1987: 103), and he avoids mirrors to avoid the revelations that are realized in seeing his face veiled. 'With self-shudderings and outward terrors, he walked continually in its shadow, groping darkly within his own soul, or gazing through a medium that saddened the whole world' (1987: 104). The veil reveals inwardness and the fear and trembling accompanying such inwardness not just to Hooper behind the veil, but also to all who come face-to-face with it, as it were. As he is entombed in that 'saddest of all prisons, his own heart' (1987: 105) so, he reveals that same prison in others who would prefer to avoid it.

I want in particular here to illustrate the educational and formative relationship between death and the veil in Hawthorne's story for it illustrates vividly the life and death struggle and the master and slave relation in the

Phenomenology of Spirit. This will be examined in more detail in a moment, but for now, note how the veil comes to symbolize death by reminding the parishioners of their existential form, and of its fragility to investigation, and how, accompanying this fragility, is the darkness of what is not revealed about themselves. As the bourgeois flees from the life and death struggle to the illusory stability of identity and independence, so, the veil uncovers the instability of this illusion and reveals the presence of death in life to the masters.

There is a further important Hegelian aspect that can be uncovered here. The parishioners were content with the face-to-face, but not because it ensured openness or that, to introduce a Levinasian theme here, it spoke of the inscrutability of God in the face of the stranger. In fact, the situation is the reverse. The face-to-face offered the mutuality only of a deception shared by the participants. The face-to-face hides more than it reveals. Only when the face-to-face was interrupted, when the veil itself refused the mutuality of its face with the face of the other, did the parishioners' philosophical education truly begin. Refused the mirror of mastery the parishioners were thrown back upon the oldest and most terrifying maxim of the Western philosophical tradition: Know Thyself.

Rousseau and civil society

This education, then, has its origins long before its modern form and content. Nevertheless, it is this modern form and content that we are concerned with here. The intrigue of the bourgeois is wonderfully exposed by Rousseau both in the *Discourses* and in *Emile*, and this is all the more important in the way Rousseau ties this intrigue to social relations and to private property in particular. We will spend a moment exploring Rousseau's critique of the mask of the bourgeois, before turning our attention to Hegel.

In the 'Discourse on the Origin of Inequality', Rousseau links the origin of the person in society to the establishing of property relations. 'The first man who, having enclosed a piece of ground, bethought himself of saying "This is mine", and found people simple enough to believe him, was the real founder of civil society' (1973: 84).

Private property for Rousseau was merely a false or inauthentic expression of the instinct for self-preservation which characterized 'natural man'. In the 'Second Discourse', he argues that it was this desire for self-preservation that led natural man to the understanding that co-operation with others aided self-preservation. The selfishness of natural man was mutual, and therefore brought about self-motivated co-operative forms of living. Such a union was a natural union, for it was based solely upon the desire for the self-preservation of each individual. For Rousseau, such a union was not yet a social union, and natural man who co-operated with other such men was not yet a person.

The natural union becomes a social union through the influence of the common life which natural man begins to lead. What was formed in order to best preserve the independence of natural man now turns against its original purpose and creates all of the social customs to which the individual loses his independence. These include speech, feelings of love, the family, leisure time and most importantly, public esteem. 'Each one began to consider the rest, and to wish to be considered in turn; and thus a value came to be attached to public esteem' (1973: 90). In the leisure time brought about through the efficiency of co-operation, natural man came to judge himself in comparison with others around him. As a result, natural self-preservation was turned into social self-interest. Independence ceased to be natural. Now man was preserved not only through self-preservation of the body, but also his identity was preserved through and by the good opinion held of him by others. In these social relations of dependency, for Rousseau, lay the origin of property and inequality.

> So long as they undertook only what a single person could accomplish, and confined themselves to such arts as did not require the joint labour of several hands, they lived free, healthy, honest, and happy lives. . . . But from the moment one man began to stand in need of the help of another; from the moment it appeared advantageous to any one man to have enough provision for two, equality disappeared, property was introduced, work became indispensable. . . . (1973: 92)

In this social situation, it was no longer the case that man worked for himself and in the interests of pure self-preservation. Now, through property, it became possible for some not to have to work at all, while others had absolutely no choice but to work for those who had 'provision for two' (1973: 92). Rousseau notes that 'in this state of affairs, equality might have been sustained, had the talents of individuals been equal' (1973: 94). However, with the disappearance of the independence of natural man, and his dependence upon others, there was now nothing to prevent the natural inequality between men unfolding, and becoming a social inequality. Strength, skill and ingenuity made equal work into unequal reward, one man gaining 'a great deal by his work, while the other could hardly support himself' (1973: 94–95).

This social inequality, made possible by the division of labour and private property, gave rise to a whole new way of life which Rousseau knows as 'civil society'. It became in the interests of men to secure co-operation with others in order to gain advantage over them, to make someone work not for the benefit of himself, but for another. To this end civil man invented new strategies to ensure his own success at the expense of others.

> Insatiable ambition, the thirst of raising their respective fortunes, not so much from real want as from the desire to surpass others, inspired all men with a vile propensity to injure one another, and with a secret jealousy, which is the more dangerous, as it puts on a mask of benevolence, to carry its point with greater security. In a word, there arose rivalry and competition on the one hand, and conflicting interests on the other, together with a secret desire on both of profiting at the expense of others. All these evils were the first effects of property, and the inseparable attendants of growing inequality. (1973: 96)

Property therefore gave rise to a society where each was at war with the other, a war masked by the pretence of 'civility'. So often seen as the natural state of man, for Rousseau this war of all against all was a corruption of natural man, a corruption inevitably brought about when one man co-operated with another for reasons other than his own self-preservation. To be able to have more than was necessary for self-preservation, and to see the advantages over others of doing so, were the beginnings of the evils of civil society. The *coup de grâce* was achieved when the right to inequality was enshrined in the universal right of private property. Rousseau argues that the rich realized quickly that the force by which they had appropriated their riches was a force that others could use against them. To secure themselves from such usurpation, the rich 'conceived at length the profoundest plan that ever entered the mind of man' (1973: 98). Masking the benefit which such a plan gave the rich, they argued to all those who had less and were a threat,

> let us join . . . to guard the weak from oppression, to restrain the ambitious, and secure to every man the possession of what belongs to him: let us institute rules of justice and peace, to which all without exception may be obliged to conform; rules that may in some measure make amends for the caprices of fortune, by subjecting equally the powerful and the weak to the observance of reciprocal obligations. (1973: 98)

The ruse was successful, for the weak were also busy trying to gain rewards for themselves, and saw in political institutions at least some advantage to their attempts. What they did not see was how the law served to ensure that social inequality was preserved, and mitigated against their own attempts for riches. 'All ran headlong to their chains' (1973: 99), unable to see through the now transparent and thus hidden mask of political equality how law enshrined social inequality. Rousseau concludes on the origin of civil society that it

> bound new fetters on the poor, and gave new powers to the rich; which irretrievably destroyed natural liberty, eternally fixed the law of property and inequality, converted clever usurpation into unalterable right, and, for the advantage of a few ambitious individuals, subjected all mankind to perpetual labour, slavery, and wretchedness. (1973: 99)

In the social relation of private property the natural need that each has of the other is distorted into the need of one to exploit the other. The strength of the independent natural man is overcome in civil society by the weakness of dependent man who seeks to exploit that need. The honesty of self-preservation is replaced by the deceit of self-interest. Natural man is replaced by social man, or by the property-owning person, and all the inequalities which are maintained in his name.

This person is related to other persons by way of exploitation. Because each person is potentially a way of another gaining self-advantage, personal relations are characterized by falsity and by deceit. It is here that the theme introduced by the veil in Hawthorne's story finds expression in Rousseau. However, while in Hawthorne the veil is visible and therefore reveals a secret behind it, in Rousseau the veil of social equality is transparent and thus reveals neither itself nor what it achieves. Now, in civil society it became in the interests of men 'to appear what they really were not. To be and to seem became two totally different things' (Rousseau, 1973: 95). In social relations the person becomes a mere illusion of 'sociability', for public life is a pretence, and is wholly artificial. Behind the civility lies the selfishness and greed of the person who works solely for his own self-interest. But unless the mask is revealed, then, like the law, it hides the real inequality behind the merely formal assurances of equality. Rousseau writes that before civil society, 'men found their security in the ease with which they could see through one another' (1973: 6). In civil society, enjoying social relations based upon private property, that artless and candid life has vanished, and every person is now merely a false show and an appearance.

> We no longer dare seem what we really are, but lie under a perpetual restraint . . . we never know with whom we have to deal. . . . What a train

of vices must attend this uncertainty! Sincere friendship, real esteem, and perfect confidence are banished from among men. Jealousy, suspicion, fear, coldness, reserve, hate, and fraud lie constantly concealed under that uniform and deceitful veil of politeness. (1973: 6–7)

The falsity of the person is what Rousseau calls *amour-propre*, a self-interest which is fed through the degree to which another can be exploited, be it in terms of material riches or personal aggrandizement. The ingenuousness of natural man Rousseau calls *amour-de-soi*, 'a natural feeling which leads every animal to look to its own preservation, and which, guided in man by reason and modified by compassion, creates humanity and virtue' (1973: 73). The formal equality of civil society masks the fact that it, in turn, masks how natural inequalities have been institutionalized. The formal relationship of one person to another invisibly masks the fact that each is out to get from the other as much advantage as it can. In the market-place advantage is sought by exploiting the needs of others, yet giving the appearance of fairness. In social relations advantage is secured by constructing an appearance of civility and compassion which will gain social favour. In both relations, the person is forced to behave in a deceitful and hypocritical way. Rousseau sees *amour-propre* as the embodiment of the fall of natural man from self-preservation to social self-interest. The cause of the fall is not man's nature, but the nature of society. It is the social relation which has turned man from an honest and open human being to a cunning and artificial person.

Two hundred and fifty years later the manner of this *amour-propre* may have changed, and few now defend the view that society is overly polite and respectful. But if Rousseau is right, then the respect that has been lost and to which some may yearn for a return, was not respect at all, only a sham, a show without integrity or substance, in reality, a transparent and therefore invisible veil masking by its transparency deceit and intrigue. Rousseau wrote *Emile* to illustrate what an education in *amour-de-soi* would be, that is, an education that prevented social custom from influencing his pupil, so that Emile's needs would always be genuine and never based on the false needs created in the veiled society. This means an education for Emile that, while it takes place in society, remains separate and detached from it until such time as Emile can participate in social relations as his own man with self-determined needs. *Emile*, therefore, is an education against the development of an invisible veil, and for a genuine and naturally developed education whose goal is to know thyself. However, even here, education against the veil is itself veiled, for Rousseau as tutor must hide from his pupil not only the way he engineers situations for Emile, but also that he is tutoring him at all. Natural education in Rousseau is also aporetic. It is a veiled education against the veil.

If politeness and ceremony are no longer the form of the bourgeois veil, nevertheless the fact of the veil persists in civil society. Here the sphere of the equality of the rights of all persons masks its more fundamental character as the sphere of selfish interests, greed, economic power and business interests that transcend even the boundaries of the nation-state. The idea of globalization speaks here of a global civil society where self-interest on the world stage has developed faster even than the veil of the equality of all persons. However, as we will see a little later, it is the pedagogy of the master still, not only to hide his mastery behind the transparent veil so that he can wilfully deceive others, but also to veil from his own view the effects of his veiled mastery.

Life and death

We noted above in Hawthorne's short story how the veil was seen by those who faced it as being akin to death itself, indeed, as if the Minister and death walked hand in hand. Why should this be so? Why is hiding the face able to evoke the darkest thoughts of death? An answer to this question comes from the way Hegel sets out the relation of life and death in the *Phenomenology*, and in particular in the way life eschews death as other. Education in Hegel returns death to life by retrieving and revealing the veil that is transparent and unseen in modern social relations. This education reveals and wears the mask that is worn but hidden by the reflective self. It does not seek to remove the mask altogether for truth in Hegel is in illusion, not its being overcome.

The structure of the life and death struggle is that of education carried in recollection.[2] Death appears to be unknowable in itself for, as many have pointed out, if death is, then I am not, and if death is not, then I am. Seemingly their paths cannot cross in such a way for both to be present in each other. Yet this view is based upon the presupposition – at its peak in mediaeval philosophy – that God is unchangeable and absolutely other in relation to a thought which can only know the true mediated in thought, that is, as changeable. The same case is made for death. Death in itself is unknowable to thinking because thinking can only think death from the point of view of life, that is, as error. But phenomenology in Hegel thinks this error as its own truth, or knows the totality of the relation to error to be thinking's own truth. Put like this, life is the actuality of death for life is the being-known of death. It is how death is known at all. Life in this sense is the actuality of death, it is the 'what is' of death. To imagine death as not-life cannot be achieved without life itself. Death, then, is dependent upon life for its very being, for its existence at all. In life, we carry the truth of death with us at all times. We will examine life's dependence upon death in a moment.

Hegel makes this same case in the way he presents the life and death struggle. He describes it in the only way open to us to know death, that is, from the perspective of life. It is important to recognize this in reading the life and death struggle, for this is to concede that there is no other place to begin to know death than in life. The struggle, precisely, *is* our recollection of what is not, in what is. The struggle is the recollection of itself from where 'itself' is already the victor. When life knows death it is from the perspective that death is other than life. It excludes the perspective of the vanquished, that is, of death. It is, therefore, also a recollection of the origin of the veil in which the role of the veil in this recollection of itself is hidden. Life presents its victory over death in the form of two beings who, in facing each other, experience the possibility of their own death. When read as a chronological sequence of events, that is, when read only forwards, this meeting is viewed as a struggle for recognition. But this is the perspective of the veiled veil, that is, of life hiding what it owes to its formative relation to death, and hiding this hiding. As such, this is a version of natural law theory that posits origin from its own point of view. But, when also read backwards, the logic of recollection can expose both the complicity of the perspective of the victor in its account of its origin and its complicity in hiding this complicity in the account. Recollection, as the loss of that which it recollects, is perfectly suited to recovering the loss of death to life. In addition, it is the method of knowing origin because what is known as origin is recollection of what is lost. This is the philosophy of origin in Hegel.

We must note here how the logic of recollection is formative and educational. It is what looks back at itself to a time when it did not know itself but must have had the potential to know itself since now it knows this potentiality as actual. This means that recollection learns of itself in the loss of itself. This is the speculative import of its negative structure, and is why and how it can know death, for it is the actuality of death, and has death as a formative part of its own truth. In recollecting the part that death plays in the victory of life recollection views the veil that hides it, and that hides itself. Recollection does not overcome the veil for it is of the veil. It does, however, open up a different account of the relation of life and death to that offered by life, and one that will know how to retrieve life's now missing combatant.

Thus, in this new account, life faces life, and experiences the negation of its immediate totality. It experiences this as the possibility that because of the 'other' (it is at this moment learning the otherness of what will become 'other') the life of this one life is neither exclusive, nor impregnable, nor certain. The desire for life, therefore, includes at this moment the death of that which has fragmented its certainty. But they are the same moment. The experience of death is also the desire for its death, for the death of death, and that means the death of life's other. Therefore, loss, death and other are all part of this one experience for life. But, of course, the other that faces life here is also life. Life is related to itself in this experience, but life does not survive this encounter as a self-relation, but as self without relation. Loss, death and other become other to this life that is now an I. It is the eschewal of death here that determines the certainty of this life as a self-conscious person. The vulnerability to and the otherness of death is here removed completely from the certainty of the I and transferred to that which has death as its own truth. The other is defined here as that which is other than life and which has death as its own truth. Life's eschewal of death is the source of all otherness, and is the illusory source also of its own political identity and certainty.

Master and slave

One common reading of Hegel at this point sees the result of the experience of death by life as a mutual recognition where each life recognizes his mutuality in the other life that faces him, and comprehends that this mutuality be expressed in some form of social contract, where each is recognized as the same as the other. But this is not the significance of the life and death struggle. Such a view of mutual recognition imposes a middle between the combatants that is wholly abstracted from the way each experiences the significance of their struggle for survival. Mutuality is a fetish of the middle of the life and death struggle, and has nothing to do with the actual shapes that this fear-of-death-become-life-and-its-other now takes. Rather, the two living beings learn about themselves from within the components of the life and death struggle. Their vulnerability now takes political form, and the life and death struggle is continued now by different means.

The life that is certain of itself is the political master. The life that must carry the death that the master has eschewed for himself is the slave. These are the shapes that life, death and other take in the first face-to-face. The only proof of this face-to-face ever happening comes in its recollection. Indeed, recollection is the actuality of this face-to-face. It knows the encounter as loss,

as impossibility, as the 'nature' of the political, and as its potential freedom
become actual. Even the risking of the lives of the combatants in the life
and death struggle is known only retrospectively by that which survives the
encounter. There is no mutual recognition in the recollection of the life
and death struggle. There is only life and death, master and slave. What lies
ahead for recollection here is to wear the veil that will reveal life and death
as death in life and life in death. In turn, this will mean learning how modern political freedom is grounded in the self that has death as other, and
that therein masks its true grounding in loss, in the trauma and fragility of
the bourgeois self. It is to the modern form that politics takes here that we
will turn in a moment.

We saw above how death was carried in and by life which nevertheless
masks what it bears. This creates the illusion that life is its own ground,
sovereign in its ubiquity and always something other than nothing. Now we
will see how the same illusion works in the master/slave relation that constitutes modern free subjectivity. The master/slave relation is the structure of
life becoming its own object in thought. Having learned from the loss of its
immediate certainty that it can absolutely vanish, life becomes known to
itself in the recollection of the struggle that it has emerged from. This
knowing is grounded in the illusion that this life is not dependent upon the
life and death struggle, but is independent and sovereign in its own right.
This illusion is the master. However, death is present in the determination
of the master, but it is present only as that which is eschewed by the master
as other than his truth. This is a crucial moment in the formation of life in
and as the reflective subject who knows himself. There is a part of his determination that is hidden from him behind the presupposition that he, the
master, has about his own sovereignty as a self. Where, then, does death
have its actuality in its relationship to life. Death is that which is prejudged
as antithetical to the existing I. Death, eschewed as a player in the identity
of the master, is posited as 'other' to this identity. For the master, death, or
the other, is the slave. The slave has no sovereignty: indeed he has no life
that can be said to be his own. He is a living death, the other to the autonomy of the master, or of life. There are themes here, then, in the master/slave
relation, that relate to the veil, to life, to death, to loss and to the other that
can now be constructed in such a way as to produce a philosophy of the
other. Furthermore, this philosophy of the other will show how the knowing of self and other is essentially *education*.

The politics of eschewing death as other, and as actual in the nothingness
of the slave, can be brought out more clearly if its opposition is presented
less abstractly and more personally. The reflective living subject that has its

actuality in and for itself is the bourgeois subject. He is his own object, and thus an end in himself. This autonomy provides for his legal identity granted to himself in his own image. Thus, the law of private property is the form of universality that enshrines this particular misrecognition of the life and death struggle. It defines sovereignty as the independence of a life and grants sovereignty to each independent form that life takes, and it defines non-sovereignty as that which lacks this self-defining independence, granting the rights of non-sovereignty to that which carries the nothingness of death with it, that is, both to inanimate objects and to those men judged as objects, that is, slaves. Presented in this way the eschewing of death as other than the living subject appears as anything but a neutral judgement. It is a judgement of the most intense political self-interest and is the actuality of the political power of the master.

The master practises a deceit here. He knows he is his own object for this self-consciousness grounds his autonomy and freedom. As such, he keeps for himself what is positive here, and gets rid of the negative implications of his objectivity. Positively, as object in itself, he is his own master. But negatively, as object for himself, he is the loss of mastery to mediation, to its being known. This one experience has ambivalence at its core. Rather than live with ambivalence the master is able to export the negativity of self-consciousness to something judged as other than his self-consciousness. He keeps his power by exporting the loss of power. It is the case, here, that such a master, in holding on to only the aspects of self-consciousness that are favourable to him, has in fact only built his house on sand. What he exports will remind him, in anxiety and fear, that he is always vulnerable to negation, for even though he thinks he is rid of it, it is still part of the totality of his identity. He exports death to others, but the exporting is always, also, his own repeated experience of vulnerability, that is, of death.

Death, then, as other to life, is always present in the affirmations that life makes about itself. How death is recognized in life determines the form of property law and of social relations. In the modern bourgeois law of private property death is the other-than-autonomous-form-of-life-known-as-I. This master, as we saw, has objects as other to it. The abolition of the slave as a legal concept is the recognition by the master that differentiating animate life into men and objects, based for example on skin colour, is not only an arbitrary judgement of power, but also an hypocritical one. As such, the rights of mastery are extended to all persons in the modern state, and the otherness of death is now only exported from them to inanimate objects and to animals.[3] But this modern, legally recognized, Western master must pay a heavy price for the freedom that life grants itself from death.

Because the Western self is not other, *no one* is other. If none are other to themselves or to each other then each has a more fulfilling life with objects, which are still other and can still therefore reinforce the certainty of the master, than they have with other masters. Since, here, no one is other, no one has any true relation to himself or to other such selves. This is the civil society of the individual rights granted to atomistic individuals who, unrelated to themselves, are also unrelated to everyone else. The only otherness they share is an otherness carried in the objects they own. As such, this man of civil society does not just relate to himself and to others as objects, he relates to objects as if they were the proof of his humanity.

This is, of course, the commodification and objectification of social relationships. The master, in exporting negation, exports the part of himself that he judges as other than mastery, precisely that part of him that is needed in order to learn of humanity from within the sovereignty of the I. Marx has shown how the capitalist market place offers only the illusion of freedom in that the free wage-labourer can still be paid to carry the negative aspects of bourgeois self-identity. But the global capitalist market means that even this wage-labourer can export elements of this negativity to others in poorer parts of the world when participating in the freedoms of, for example, shopping and travel. As Chapter 3 will argue in more detail, these freedoms, stripped of negativity, become actions without implication. Education in Hegel aims for the retrieval of this implication as complicity, from which negativity may be retrieved for the conception of humanity.

Self and other

I want now to place the experience of the actuality of death in life within the relation of self and other in order to draw out Hegel's philosophy of the other. In short, I will present the case for the other in Hegel as the loss that is carried by the self, but carried behind an invisible veil that holds the reality of the self and other grounded in (their) illusion. Recognizing how illusion determines the identity of the self and the other is an education into the way loss – in this case of sovereignty – is formative.

Thus far, we have explored the relation of self and other as the misrecognition of the life and death struggle, and of death in life in particular, and as a misrecognition hidden by the definition of freedom that it makes possible. What remains is to translate this now into a philosophy of the other, which requires, in turn, the formulation of the concept of the other. In short, the other is that which is present in the self as loss. Models of the other that are grounded in an equality of pluralism only suppress the experience of the other in the self and thus have to assert it over and above that experience. Pluralism is the equality of masters, often, of course, asserted over those who are not masters. This is the equality, for example, of the global market. Models of the other that are grounded in a radical heterogeneity, be it difference or otherwise-than-being, assert the experience of the other over that of the self. This, too, hides a mastery, but in this case it is not the mastery of the self, but mastery over the self. Education in Hegel holds both aspects of this experience of the opposition of equality and difference in tension, and finds a philosophy of the other therein.

There are two aspects that constitute the triadic education of self and other. The self is other to himself internally and externally, but in such a way that both the internal and the external relation of self and other educate each other. We have seen this same relation in action between life and death, and between master and slave. Now we will explore it as the education of self and other. The self in question here is still the bourgeois master. This self is determined in and by the relation of life to death which has actuality as the master and the slave. The self, therefore, in the same way has his identity formed by exporting death, or that which is other than his self-certainty, to anything that is not himself. The self is grounded in a loss that he is not yet aware of internally as being part of his own determination. Loss becomes other therefore only in an external sense, and inwardly the self is without the threat of loss, without the danger to it of what is other.

Having exported otherness, however, the self has already sown the seeds of his own negation, for that which he has eschewed nevertheless remains, albeit suppressed, as constitutive of the identity of the self. This self has laid the ground externally for an education about himself internally. This education, as we will see now, is both revolution and re-formation[4]. It is revolution because negation will return from externality to the source of its eschewal; and it is re-formation because this return is an experience in which what returns to itself is changed in doing so. It is this experience that generates the concept of the other.

As death was judged other to life by life, so loss is judged other to self by self. The self has exported its vulnerability and as such appears immune to dependence upon anything other than itself. This is the ground of its sovereignty. It is the educative significance of loss in this sovereignty that elicits the philosophy of the other, and it is to the structure of this education that we now turn.

The tautology of the self is that the self is defined as not other. This has two aspects. First, the self as the I is not other to itself because otherness is grounded in what is not the I. Second, the self, because it is I, is also not the other that exists heteronomously, that is, it is not the other who is slave, or animal or object, nor is it the other person because, as sovereign, these persons are indifferent to each other. Thus, the I is not other both internally and externally. However, education in Hegel knows the educative significance for the I in this certainty that it is not other. The certainty of the I and the loss of certainty as otherness cannot (yet) find themselves in each other. *But* the certainty of the self is so only relative to the other. This is already foreclosed in saying that the certainty of the I is that it is not other. The I is defined positively by being defined negatively, that is, against what it is not. That the I is not the other means that the I is only in relation to what it is not. This is the first element of the experience that constitutes the philosophy of the other. He does not yet understand that this is the same otherness that he exported from himself. But this experience of the vulnerability of self-certainty, of the loss of certainty to uncertainty and of independence to dependence, is the beginning of wisdom. The self is now known, in fear and trembling, as the opposite of what it took itself to be.

The second experience sees the self come to learn that this vulnerability has a name and a truth of its own. The name of this vulnerability of the self is the other, because it is this other to which the self is indebted for his own identity. The self here is no longer immune to his own aporetic identity. Rather, he is made to suffer by that which he thought he had eschewed, namely, otherness to the identity of the life called I. The truth of this vulnerability is even more powerful because its truth is the opposite of the truth that the self assumed for itself. The truth of the self who is not other is now the truth of the self who is not self.

If the philosophy of the other consisted only in the radical instability of the self, then life might well be called *différance*. Alternatively, if the difference of self and other is reconciled in being understood, then life might be called mutual recognition. But the loss of the truth of the self is not the overcoming of the self, nor is it the not overcoming of the self. It is rather the *Aufhebung* of the self, and that means that what is lost is also retained, and that this loss and retention between them form a further relation that re-forms – is the re-formation of – that first relation. Neither loss nor self are overcome and somehow left behind. Their re-formed relation is proof of their persistence for they are the component parts of this re-formation. This we must now explore as the third partner in the philosophy of the other.

The self that is not self is having returned to it that which it thought constituted no part of itself, that is, its vulnerability to otherness. Now it finds vulnerability at its core. But in addition it finds that this internal vulnerability also has an external existence. Since vulnerability was other to the self, vulnerability exists in everything that was deemed as other to the self by the self. Death was other than life, slave other than master, and now otherness *per se* is other than the self. The truth of loss that now pervades the self has an objective existence outside of himself. This truth is none other than that which was the part of the formation of the self that the self discarded. His arrogance is coming back to haunt him. His new truth as not-self is found to have a real existence as what is not self. Thus, self and other are related to each other once again. We should not say that they are re-united for they were never united. As recollection death was always other. But we can say that a relation is formed between them in the experience that the self has had of his loss of certainty and of this loss being in the world as what is other to himself. They are the same truth, but they are this same truth only in and as the education of the self. Their relation is existent only in this education because in education, and indeed, as education, the ambiguity of this relation is its own truth.

Education in Hegel can hold negations together because education in Hegel is the self-formative circle of the same returning to itself and making a difference in doing so. It is in such self-determining opposition that learning appears as both subject and substance. Only this philosophical learning can have loss as self-development, self-education, and self-re-formation, for it has its own end in its own loss and its own loss as its own end; and both of these it has as its own revolution and re-formation. Thus, in the case of self and other that we are exploring here, self and other are not united in a mutual recognition nor differentiated as *différance* or rhizome (Deleuze). They are, however, related in an experience of their shared negativity such that the truth of the self as not self, and the truth of other as not self, become formative of the self whose experience this is. The self here learns the truth of himself, and learns that the truth of himself is in the learning. He cannot become the other, for it is still the self that is having this learning experience. He cannot not be the other either, for that loss is now integral to his own identity. If he cannot be the other and cannot not be the other, what is he? He is the education carried in the triadic phenomenology of aporetic identity.

The educative significance of this aporetic experience of self and other is the philosophy of the other. It is the concept, the knowing, of the other by the self. The difficulty of this education is captured by the following phrase: I am already other and the other is not me. I am already other because the certainty of my self-identity is already defined against that which is other than this living I. The second half of the phrase – the other is not me – contains the substance of the education that grounds the philosophy of the other. On the one hand, the other is not *me*, but on the other hand, the other *is* not me. If we add a hyphen to the last two words the meaning becomes clearer; the other *is* (the I that is already) not-me. Since the self is already not itself, not-me, and the other is also not me, the self and the other are the same in their difference. That which was exported by the self cannot be returned to it in any pure form; it is too late for that. But the self can see the meaning and the significance for it of having done so. It has returned to itself the part of itself that it eschewed, that is, what is experienced as loss is returned to it also *as* loss; what is experienced as vulnerability is returned to it also as vulnerability. The lack of unity in the relation of loss to itself is the actuality of the other to the modern bourgeois self. 'I am already other and the other is not me' is a statement of the actuality of the modern relation of self and other, an actuality that has to be thought if the misrecognition of self and other, and of life and death, are to have any formative social, political and philosophical import.[5] It is to this import that we turn now in the final two sections of this chapter.

Living death

I want to explore a little the education that philosophy can carry regarding the origin of the I in the life and death struggle. As we saw above, the veil worn by the Minister walked hand in hand with death. Why should this be so? It is because the veil is the truth of death in life. When the face-to-face becomes face-to-veil, as it did for the Minister's parishioners, the face has reflected back to it the veil that it also wears, the veil that is, however, transparent and that is seen through but not also seen. It takes the veil to come face-to-face with itself for the veil to become visible. But what, then, is the relation to death here? Following on from the life and death struggle just presented, life has to learn of itself and of the truth of itself from its experience of being finite and of being able to die, to vanish completely. Life that presents itself as master holds itself apart from its relation to death, for mastery is the export of death to the life of another. This is mastery; not over death itself (although this is part of its illusion) but over its relation to death in life. The veil of the master is transparent but present. It veils the death that stalks his certainty. When this transparent veil of self-delusion is exchanged for a real veil, the wearer reveals the uncertainty of the master. He reveals it to himself, for he knows he is acknowledging his absolute vulnerability. He becomes absolutely vulnerable because he can no longer present to others a transparent veil of his certainty; and he reveals it to others for they see their own veil, their own illusory certainties, now revealed by his veil. The veiled face-to-face reveals the truth in a way that the face-to-face never can. This stands as a political critique of the face-to-face in Levinas. There is no such face-to-face that is not mediated by the transparent veil of mastery or by the prior face-to-face of life and death. The claim for the breaking through of God into earthly identity does not pay sufficient respect to the power of life to sustain us in our identity. I may care, even weep for the suffering of others, but always from behind my veil. Only in exposing and wearing my veil am I really face-to-face.[6]

Where, then, might we look for the presence of death carried in life? We saw in the struggle how life learns of itself only in the experience of its being abolished in death. The truth of life here is of the recollection of itself as pure vulnerability, but as not (yet) dead. As Hegel says, absolute negation is not for those who survive the struggle, but it is, nevertheless, the truth of their survival. Where in life, then, is this recollection an education about the truth of life? It can be found in the sadness of facing death. It is in sadness that recollection as the actuality of death meets its always absent and always present teacher, but this experience of sadness reforms sadness into something substantial, for sadness is the recollection of death in life. The mourners are strangely comforted.

Philosophy knows this. It knows how the life and death struggle is carried in each life and has its unity and difference in each individual. The individual so often only recognizes this in extreme situations where death is seen to be close. It can be a lover, a relation, a public figure, even a princess. The death of any loved one, ours or someone else's, raises the philosophical recognition of the presence of death in our life and existence. The bereaved acts here as spiritual ambassador for the truth, able to educate all who see in him their own relation to the true, that is, to absolute vulnerability.[7]

More generally, when someone dies, and we are in contact (in whatever way) with that death, we are educated about life. I do not mean here to restrict myself to Kierkegaard's observation that we will all die at some time and that the sooner we realize this, the better – although of course he is right. The more subtle point Kierkegaard makes is not live now, for tomorrow we die. It is rather that we should carry death with us as teacher. But I want to extend Kierkegaard's observation here. Being close to the death of another we are reminded of how death is constitutive of ourselves. Philosophy knows sadness as negation and as the uncertainty, anxiety and doubt that accompanies the deepest questions about who we are and why we are here. Philosophy, as the presence of doubt, is also the presence of

death as teacher. Philosophy knows the I that is not I, but knows it forma-
tively, as an education. The protection against this education is the
appearance of the I as independent, free and without guile in its identity.
This appearance is the transparency of the veil that hides the not I and
hides this hiding. But the veil cannot always remain hidden, especially when
it meets the death of those close to it. At the funeral of a loved one we are
mostly death, we are not I at a deep level of prescience, at least for a time.
The death of the loved one brings us closer to the loved one even than in
life, for we are not I as he or she is not I. Negative meets negative in this life
and death struggle. Here there is the mutuality of death with death. And
this is positive. The truth of the bereaved, on such occasions, becomes
death as our own truth. He or she re-minds us of the way death, negatively,
is constitutive already of our life as human beings. This is the way in which
the sadness of funerals can be enjoyed as life-affirming, that is, education-
ally at a profound spiritual level. Sadness is the name of the truth, and
philosophy is its means of inspiring comprehension or recollection. It is, in
Hegel's language, where the slave is his own work, a living death. This same
truth, as we will see below, constitutes what Hegel calls world spirit.

Living death seen in this way clearly raises the political question about
how one should relate to the other, be it other in colour, gender, age, race,
sexuality, religion, culture, nation, or whatever. The freedom of pluralism
also wears the veil of political transparency. Power requires to be read into
the relation of self and other, not out of it, if the truth that it carries is to be
open to its being learned.[8] One recognizes here the caution that is needed.
To criticize pluralism looks as if it might be advocating inequality, or even
practising prejudice and discrimination. On the contrary, what it commends is that the actuality of inequality not be suppressed or hidden.
Inequality between self and other is a structural feature of their political
relationship. It does not cancel itself just because it works both ways because,
as we have seen, their relationship is grounded in negativity and the negativity of the two selves does not add up to a whole. This lack of completion
is present whether the self affirms his difference to the other or their mutuality. The other is already the representative of the incompletion of the
relation.

Thus the political question as to how one secures justice between self and
other is translated philosophically into how one does justice to their actual
relationship. Anything else is an injustice against their recollection of their
origin and determination. Doing justice to the actuality of self and other
means retrieving the struggle that forms them. Such retrieval, in recollection, is educative in three ways. First, the self learns it is not-I. Second, this

self learns that the other is also not this I. Third, the self knows that it sustains this education. Here, then, education is a value in itself, and is the value that does justice to self and other. But even if this work and this justice are also undertaken by the other, and even though they will be the same in their difference, justice to their relation still demands that it cannot be abstracted into a middle ground. The just relation of self and other requires their truth in their struggle. Hiding the struggle by assertions of sameness or difference is only an illusory justice. To really do justice to the difference of the other one must also do justice to the other in oneself. The relation is both of these struggles.

World spirit

World spirit might well be the most difficult and contentious element of Hegelian philosophy. If it is understood without being grounded in education in Hegel then it is reduced to a statement of imperialism seemingly advocating that the West drag the rest of the world into modernity, justified because this will be rational progress. We will explore in more detail the way this unfolds in the history of philosophy in the following chapter. Against such views we can read world spirit as education in Hegel, and in particular as constituted by the philosophy of the other that we have just described. What is at stake here regarding world spirit is nothing less than the idea of humanity known and understood as the actuality of the relation of self and other on the world stage. It is where education in Hegel achieves global significance. Again here we will interweave the themes of the veil, life, death, loss and vulnerability around the relation of self and other in order to present world spirit as education in Hegel.

As we saw above, life, in asserting its identity in a certainty immune to its own aporetic grounding, excludes death as other than identity. Death is the negation in which life begins its self-conscious existence, but its contribution to this formative experience is eschewed. It is not hard to see how the certainty of the Western self repeats this eschewal in order to shield it from its own vulnerabilities. Rather than learn of itself from the other, it prefers to protect the illusions of its certainties. It does this by many means, all of which have in common the export of negation, that is, of fear, vulnerability and death, to those who are other than itself. At one extreme, when fear of death in life is total, when it is fear lacking fear and is without mediation or learning, then it seeks to secure itself in the idolatry of uniforms and scapegoats. Lacking mediation it is free to export total negation, free, that is, to export death without the negation of the self of the exporter. At its furthest limit, this is genocide. Evil lives in such privation of education.

But even without the totality of uniforms and scapegoats what chance has the other, the stranger, if we – and here 'we' should not be avoided, because it reveals the hidden veil of Western self-interest – if we do not know at whom we gaze because we suppress self-gaze? Modernity is not just out-sourcing its call centres. It is exporting fear and vulnerability in the form of conflict and instability to ensure that they are not ours.

After all, who is the easier to bomb? Is it the other who is undecideable or otherwise-than-being, yet-to-come, and beyond comprehension, *or* is it the other that I find in myself as the truth of my own vulnerability? Is not the answer here in fact that it is the unknowable and incommensurable other who is expendable, since he is not recognized as my own humanity? To know thyself in the sense carried within Hegel's philosophy of the other is not a Western logocentric ontotheological imperialism. On the contrary, the refusal to know thyself is the domination of abstract reason over its own grounding in death, loss and vulnerability. Knowing thyself is the disrup-tion of that abstract domination. It is an education wherein what I learn of myself is also what I learn of the otherness that constitutes my vulnerable identity. Neither is this solipsism. Solipsism is where the I refuses its own relation and refuses its negation, and refuses the implications for it of this negation. To refuse to know thyself is to refuse to know the other. This is the refusal that finds it easier to drop bombs.

Thus, there is no stranger who is not already known to me, and there is no self that is not already lost to me. This is the concept of the other in modernity. In the concept of the other he and I are the same in our differ-ence, and justice must always be done to the difference for the same to be sustained, and to the same for difference to be sustained. The other is not me; the other, therefore, is also me in my vulnerable non-sovereignty. The 'also' here is spirit because spirit is the return and reform of the relation of sovereignty and non-sovereignty in and as human education. Spirit is the learning of vulnerability and is the vulnerability of this learning. When the 'also' refers to the otherness of the idea of *humanity* this is world spirit in education in Hegel.

Indeed, this 'also' currently takes shape in the bombs that carry the export of otherness beyond the West, and in the cheap commodities that return it seemingly without implication for our vulnerability.[9] But world spirit knows this exporting of vulnerability and importing of security philosophically, that is, as its own formative experience and education. It knows the vulnera-bility that motivates the export and it knows the fear and trembling that comes with the import. The education carried in world spirit is not just a vulnerability of nation states to each other. It is also the vulnerability of the consequences and implications of a life-style that discards such consequences and implications as far away as is politically and technologically possible. To learn to see the relation of freedom (of life-style) to death is to learn to risk the education of the self regarding its relation to itself and its other. The actuality of this education will be sadness. Sadness registers my experience of the other who must suffer for my security, and it registers also my resignation at the intractability of this suffering. If sadness is all that can be learned here, then there is no truth to it, for it would mean that there is no educative import to the sadness, that we learn nothing from it. But because the relation between my not-self and the other who is not me, *is* (not-me), this sadness has formative significance. If we restrict world spirit to life and death, to feelings of sadness, we are avoiding the actuality of sadness, and we are avoiding its political education. We are avoiding being changed by the truth that presents itself in sadness.

However, we cannot ignore the importance that the distance of self and other has on this education. The further away death is from us, in time as in space, then the less powerful becomes its truth. There are more tears shed for the local death with universal significance than for the universal significance of the death local to somewhere else. How is the return of death to realize itself as world spirit when its truth exhausts itself the further it has to travel? Our answer here can be that the return is carried in our philosophical education, for it is in philosophy that the education of self and other has actuality. It is where modernity carries its negative truth knowingly and with comprehension about its relation to the other. Modernity's un-philosophical masters have eschewed their own philosophical education. Even the hypocrisy of legitimate death – collateral damage – and illegitimate death – innocent victims – has not revealed to them the veil of mastery, worn invisibly, that kills the meaning of death, and kills the other carried in it.

How hard is it, then, to be in the truth of the relation of self and other, whether between and within persons, cultures, communities, or the nations that constitute the political totality of the earth? It is hard in proportion to the extent to which the relation to one's death in and by negation is characterized by its suppression, its eschewal and its denial. The greater the extent to which fears and insecurities are pushed on to others, at home, abroad, and soon no doubt, into space, the less is the self sufficiently educated to be able to meet them in the truth of the encounter. It is in education's own subjectivity and substance – its revolution and reform of itself – that the singular can also be universal, can also know the other. This is to learn otherness as the truth of the self in the difficulty of remaining the self who is vulnerable to this truth. Known as having its truth in this education, and contra both the abstract post-foundational claims for undecideability and the excesses of the standpoint of mutual recognition, the concept of the other reclaims all the imperial terms again: 'our', 'we', 'West', 'logos', 'I', 'reason', 'us', 'society', 'spirit', 'absolute', 'property', 'person', etc, in order to be able to speak of otherness with the ambivalence of the complicity of mastery that it demands. The more unseen is the veil of the master, the more difficult is it to learn that I am already the other and the other is not me.

Notes

1 I first came across this story by way of Josh Cohen (2005).
2 The meaning carried by the term 'recollection' here is dealt with in more detail in Chapter 2.
3 The otherness of animals is another recent export of death to recognize itself in and as the vulnerability of the master.
4 The hyphen signals the relation here to the *Aufhebung* which, in the following chapter, is defined as self (re-)formation. See also Chapter, note 3.
5 Note here that the concept of otherness is not described as 'I am already other; the other returns to me', which would be closer to a formulation that might be inferred from Adorno and Horkheimer (1979) according to the dialectic of enlightenment. This is because the dialectic of enlightenment describes the revolution of subjectivity but not its re-formation. Thus subjectivity is famously caught in a frozen dialectic, and is the key understanding Adorno's melancholic science of negative dialectic. There may yet be further modern reasons for such melancholia.
6 This discussion of Levinas is returned to below in Chapter 5.
7 Sometimes a public figure can embody for others the truth of this living death. In thinking about this, I was watching the Ryder Cup of 2006. A golfer named Darren Clark was representing Europe against the United States. His wife had died of cancer only a few months before but he had made himself available to play. The emotions that this produced, most notably in the crowds at the K Club in Dublin, but also amongst the television audience, were precisely of the truth of living death that was embodied in him. This emotion was visible every time he appeared. Tiger Woods, a US golfer, had recently lost his own father, and the hug between the two grieving opponents was the embrace of the I that is We in sadness. And the humility felt in and for suffering is witness to this deepest of human educations.
8 This is true also of debates in social science regarding qualitative research. The way that certain qualitative research perspectives have embraced the idea that the otherness of the research object can be respected and not objectified is grounded in the veil of the veil. The freedom it appears to offer the object is a veil that hides the presuppositions of self and other that already ground the identity of both

the self of the researcher and the object of the research project as other. The self-assurance of the researcher grows in strength from both the funds she 'wins' to carry out the research and the reputation she seeks for herself in publishing the results. Here, precisely, the self of the researcher exports the uncertainty of otherness to the research object for her own ends. The more 'open' the approaches to the object become, the more invisible becomes the veil.

9 This vulnerability, since 9/11 is also being returned as bombs.

Chapter 2

Education in Hegel in the History
of Philosophy

*What then is it in the soul which causes it to take more pleasure in things which it
loves when they are found and recovered than if it has always had them?*
(Augustine, 1998: 137)

In this chapter I argue for a reassessment of the significance of education
in Hegel's history of philosophy. This focuses partly on the relation that
Aufhebung has to two other educational themes in Hegel, those of *Bildung*
and *Entwicklung*, and on the way that the educational structure of *Aufhebung*
can be understood to lie in the notion of *recollection*. The implications of this
notion of recollection in the history of philosophy are then examined in
regard to the view that the history of philosophy is explicitly a Western
imperialism and that its view of freedom is imbued with a suppression of its
'others'.

Introduction

Consider the following quotation from Hegel in the *Introduction to the
Lectures on the History of Philosophy*. On the development of philosophy over
the last two thousand years Hegel says

> The first thing is the purely abstract and universal thought . . . It is thought
> as it appears in the East and is connected with Oriental religion and the
> Oriental consciousness generally. Here thought is wholly abstract and
> substantial without any advance or development (*Entwicklung*), and
> indeed it is the same now as it was many millennia ago . . .

> The second thing is self-determining thought, the Concept; this we see
> emerging in the [Ancient] Greek world . . .

The third thing is the fixing of these differences [between thought and being, and between subject and object] and consciousness of them. This is the philosophy of the modern European world, Christian and Germanic philosophy; (1987: 174; 1940: 36–37).

And a little later on he says, 'man and God, the subjective Idea and the objective Idea are one here. This is the Germanic principle, this unification of subject and object' (1987: 179; 1940: 246).

One may well be unsettled by these assertions regarding the truth of the individual in universal modern Western philosophy. It reads like the confidence of a man who, having his essence and his truth in himself, has shut up shop to any and all other possibilities and gone home in the warm glow of self-satisfaction of a job perfectly completed. Does the following quotation do anything to mediate this apparent conceit and arrogance? It is taken (in an abbreviated form) from the final paragraph of the *Phenomenology of Spirit*. It states that spirit's becoming at home with its essence, its self-fulfilment

consists in perfectly knowing what it is, in knowing its substance. [T]his knowing is its withdrawal into itself in which it abandons its outer existence and gives its existential shape over to recollection (*Erinnerung*). . . . [This recollection is] a new shape of Spirit. In the immediacy of this new existence the Spirit has to start afresh to bring itself to maturity as if, for it, all that preceded were lost and it had learned nothing from [its earlier experiences]. But recollection (*Er-innerung*), the inwardizing, of that experience, has preserved it. . . . [Here, then] the goal, Absolute Knowing, or Spirit that knows itself as Spirit, has for its path the recollection of the [previous shapes of spirit] as they are in themselves. . . . Their preservation [combining] history . . . and the Science of Knowing . . . form alike the inwardizing and the Calvary of Absolute Spirit (1977: 492–93; 1949: 563–64, [Hegel's italics removed]).

The tone of this quotation in its description of absolute knowing is rather different from the first one. Here, absolute spirit knows itself absolutely only in and as a process of self-education. It recollects all of the mistakes that it has previously made in how it understood itself, and has those mistakes now as formative of itself. What it is now is the recollection of all that it has been. The question that poses itself here for us is what kind of an educational event is this recollection?[1] I will address this question now around

issues relating to the Hegelian history of philosophy, and in particular those
of cultural imperialism and mastery. But, in advance, my answer to these
questions lies in two further questions that are raised by the final paragraph
of the *Phenomenology*. First, how could this combination of history and learning in recollection close itself, as if it was a termination and completion,
and still be itself, still be learning? Second, how could recollection know
itself as the Calvary of absolute spirit without the renewal, the continuing
education, of itself as life in death?

Nevertheless, it is widely the case that the absolute in Hegel is received
one-sidedly as merely abstract, positive assertion. Couple such assertion on
truth with comments on some other cultures and races that Hegel makes –
including on African slaves, native Americans, Asians and Jews – and it is
perhaps unavoidable that Hegel is labelled at best as a product of his age,
and at worst as a defender of Western imperialism. This is only exemplified
by his history of philosophy and philosophy of history which seem to claim
that the West is the culmination of what reason can achieve in terms of the
state and religion and the thinking of the absolute.

It has become part of the spirit of our own age to discipline thinkers from
ages less enlightened than our own. Thus, Philip Kain has recently written
that 'we cannot pretend that Hegel confines himself to merely describing
Western ethnocentrism, imperialism, and racism . . . We must [also] admit
that Hegel actually endorses them and we must be clear that this endorse-
ment is deeply objectionable' (2005: 252).[2] Yet isn't this exactly what Hegel
is being accused of, that is, looking backwards at times less enlightened
than his own and judging their inadequacies? What will the future make of
Kain's judgement here other than perhaps that he did not recognize the
imperialisms of his own present in his comment on past imperialisms?
In fact, in education in Hegel there is a much more rigorous acknowledgement of complicity in the imperialisms of the age than there is in Kain's
reading of Hegel here. Hegelian philosophy allows no 'natural' or common
sense standpoints immunity from negation. This changes fundamentally
the status of philosophical critique in Hegel, for its own standpoint is within
this unavoidable groundlessness of autoimmunity or self-opposition. How,
for example, could one read the quotation above from the *Lectures on the
History of Philosophy* and *not* experience such oppositions? *Of course* in the
quotation we bristle at the certainties regarding European philosophy. It is
precisely in such bristling – and Hegel would have expected this – that
the standpoint commends its own autoimmunity. The notions of the beginning, the development and the consummation of Western thought in
the concept and its attendant notions of freedom that are carried in the

quotation, also carry their own negation in and by their unavoidable complicity in the social and political relations of their time. That they are *open* to this complicity absolutely and unconditionally is what sets education in Hegel apart from philosophical critique that forgets or avoids its own imperialisms, even in stating that they are not avoiding them. This is the changed meaning of knowledge and of truth in education in Hegel. It means that it is possible to critique, for example, the presuppositions and the standpoints of critiques of imperialism and racism, not with a view to supporting either imperialism or racism, far from it, but with a view to revealing how they repeat in their critiques the imperialisms that they oppose. This is how the *Aufhebung* works, not just by rejecting tyrannies, but by recognizing the tyrannies even in such rejections. The contradictions of reason cannot disown their origins in 'free' thought. This is the extra mile that education in Hegel travels, not just to expose contingency, but the contingency of the exposure. I attempt this now with regard to the history of philosophy, past and present.

Hegel's notions of education

There are three notions of education in Hegel which, together, constitute the process of the history of philosophy. These are *Bildung, Entwicklung* and *Aufhebung.*

Bildung (cultural formation)

Bildung in Hegel is formation or development through the repetition of misrecognition. This is the meaning of culture in Hegel. It prioritizes the process involved in the experience of contradictions, most especially when the particular and the universal are opposed to each other. But if *Bildung* is seen as the entire import of education in Hegel this is a mistake, not just in regard to *Bildung,* but also to the nature of Hegelian science as a whole.

At times *Bildung* is translated as 'culturation' to refer to developments that move away from nature and towards reason. In the *Philosophy of Right,* for example, *Bildung* appears in relation to the maturation of the single individual from the necessity of external needs to the freedom of internal, rational needs. Hegel rejects the idea that *Bildung* is some kind of corruption of a state of nature. Rather, *Bildung* develops the idea of the individual who has needs, but equally is able to recognize himself in these needs. Civil society is thus the enculturing of the person in his comprehension that his freedom lays in his freedom from others. This is the culture, the education, of independence. But *Bildung* will also develop the individual's understanding of the contradictions of this independence, and will therein enable the person to recognize his objectivity in the universality of the state. Hegel is clear here that this education is a hard struggle for it involves the negation of desire in and by the labour of the concept. *Bildung*, therefore, describes the process by which ethical life replaces natural need, and it is the maturation of the person from particular to universal, and of family to civil society and state.

In the *Phenomenology* and the *Lectures on the History of Philosophy* the education carried in and by *Bildung* is given a much fuller treatment. Specifically, it describes how the self-alienation of spirit is played out in the Middle Ages between the lawless barbarian invaders and the divine authority of the Christian God. The only law that is present here is the inward devotion to God. But because the political world and the spiritual world are alienated from each other there exists both appalling barbarism and austere penitence in equal measure.

However, culture (*Bildung*) holds this relationship of contradiction and opposition within itself in a way that will educate it to a recognition of its rational universality. Culture in this sense not only repeats the lack of a relation between God and man but it also experiences the failure of all attempts to unite them. All attempts to change the world according to the Will of the beyond collapse in on themselves precisely because they are *human* attempts. Such attempts are re-formed[3], then, not in succeeding with reconciliation, but rather as emphasizing, again, the impossibility of such reconciliation – yet, as we will come to see, this also reaffirms their relation to each other. The result of the experience of the repetition of opposition as failure results in even greater alienation. Doing God's Will on earth becomes ever more impossible, yet demands ever greater efforts, all of which will be repeatedly re-formed against their original intentions. The more devoted are the attempts to bring this world into line with the other world, the greater is the repetition of the experience of barbarism.

Bildung here has two contradictory motions. It reinforces the *status quo*, reproducing spirit's self-alienation in existing social relations, and yet it is changed or re-formed in doing so by the experience of this repetition. Together these constitute political experience, and the relationship of theory and practice. Reform is the goal of a political action, but it is re-formed in attempting such reform, and re-formed in such a way as to reveal the domination of existing social relations over all such political action. As we will see shortly, it is philosophy that can comprehend the meaning and significance of this experience in which the goal of political action is inverted or turned against itself.

The education of *Bildung* in the *Phenomenology* is to be found in the totality of this pre-determined formation and equally pre-determined re-formation. Its moments are those of speculative logic. It is, first, an immediate (re)production of the alienation of spirit, one that contains therein the drive for reform. Second, *Bildung* is the negative experience of attempting such reforms, that is, that they do not work and merely reinforce the *status quo*. Thus 'good' action for reform becomes 'bad' action in practising further earthly barbarism. The noble deed becomes the ignoble deed. The ruler is not an obedient servant but a wealthy and powerful master. But, and third, there is the recognition of the implications of these contradictions, that nothing is quite as it seems, and that meanings and values are themselves inverted, or pass into their opposite. Thus, says Hegel, 'the language of this disrupted consciousness is the perfect language and the authentic existent Spirit of this entire world of culture' (1977: 316; 1949: 370).

The self-contempt that results from this experience of hypocrisy is the experience of 'pure' culture, stripped now of the finery behind which power masquerades as servant to God. This is the pure culture, the pure education, of the faithful self of pure consciousness as really the reasoning schemer and deceiver who must face his own truth in the dissolving of his charades. Pure education here is the I that says I am never what I take myself to be; rather, I am the negation of all that I take myself to be. My hypocrisy is my education regarding myself. I have been reformed every time I have sought to deny this hypocrisy. Now I must accept the universality of this re-formation, that is, the universality of the negative. 'Here, then, we have the Spirit of this real world of culture. Spirit that is *conscious* of itself in its truth and in its Notion. It is this absolute and universal inversion and alienation of the actual world and of thought; it is *pure culture*' (1977: 316; 1949: 371). This alienation reforms spirit and reforms the reforming spirit. The double negation is the truth of a new shape of spirit, an honourable spirit that owns up to the hypocrisy of not acknowledging inevitable inversion. With this education the edifices built out of hypocrisy collapse. This I is now prepared for further and higher education regarding its objectivity and formation and re-formation but this, as we will see in a moment, requires a different form of philosophical education.

Bildung, then, contains within itself the totality of a dialectic that forms and is re-formed in turn. All universals are found culpable of self-interest, and self-interest becomes the new universality. This also characterizes *modern* social relations. Culture does not describe a one-off stage of spirit's alienation and education. Culture is the movement of all experiences of inversions and of contradictions in theory and practice. Modern culture expresses the separation of thought and the absolute. Here, though, it concerns the inversion of reason which is experienced as acting against itself, and takes place not in the feudal barbarism of lawlessness, but in the universal property law of bourgeois social relations. This is not the alienation of spirit where personality is to be sacrificed in bringing God's will to earth; it is rather the misrecognition of spirit as universal in individual property rights. The person of Roman law returns now with the status of Emperor shared among free men, and a free man is the man who is independent of others in owning his own property. Nevertheless, contradiction and culture are both present here. The good act that seeks universal significance becomes the act of perpetuating self-interest. Philosophical education persists in the same self-contempt for not being what the master appears to be.

Thus, to comprehend modern social relations requires acknowledging that actions for universality are determined in and by a world wherein the terms defining such actions and purposes have already ensured their incompatibility. Here is the double bind of all political action: the terms that define what must be done are the same terms that make it impossible. At this point one can imagine resignation in the face of failure and impotence. But this is not the significance of *Bildung*. *Bildung* is a totality of opposition. In *modern* terms this totality has been defined by Horkheimer and Adorno as the dialectic of enlightenment. This states the totality of inversion and contradiction as *myth is already enlightenment and enlightenment returns to myth*. In a sense this dialectic of enlightenment is pure culture, or the culture of reason wherein formation and re-formation is reason in and for itself. The dialectic of enlightenment takes culture as far as it can go, that is, to the pure recognition of itself as misrecognition. But the culture of culture contained in *Bildung* here – and in its modern form as the dialectic of enlightenment – is a philosophical education regarding the truth that this total inversion contains. This philosophical form of Hegelian education is the *Aufhebung*.

Entwicklung (development)

Entwicklung, in the *Introduction to the Lectures on the History of Philosophy*, refers to development as the unfolding and evolving of a story or a drama. In particular it is used to illustrate the relation between potentiality and actuality.

In the section entitled 'The Idea as Development' (*Die Idee als Entwicklung*)[4] Hegel teaches that in any form of development there must be two principles, namely potentiality and actuality. A development must have the potential for that development already within itself as part of itself. Spirit, then, for Hegel, is self-formative and reveals and learns only what was always potential in it.

In describing development as potential Hegel often uses the seed as illustrative. 'The seed,' he says, 'is endowed with the entire formation (*Formation*) of the plant; the productive force (*Kraft*) and the product (*Hervorgebrachte*) are one and the same. Nothing emerges except what was already present' (1987: 72–73; 1940: 103). This activity of the seed, then, is self-production (*Sich selbst Hervorbringen*; [1940: 103]). However, it is formative not just of its potential, but also of the repetition of its production beyond itself. The seed does not just produce itself once. Rather, the process of self-formation is complete only when a new seed has been produced, and therefore even the completion of the self-formation is not really a completion, only a renewal or a repetition.

This entire cycle of self-development from potential to potential has its actuality in the *existence* of the potential. If the content of the seed never waivers in its self-development, the form that this content takes in doing so nevertheless changes visibly. It has, as Hegel puts it, to become 'something different' (1987: 73) in acquiring a form in relation to other things. However, what the seed does naturally, reason must do cognitively. The seed can be all plants as one plant can be all seeds. Development here is not ruptured by relations of universal and particular, for its circular nature is without beginning or end.[5] But reason's development is not so unproblematic. Hegel notes the part reason plays in the development or unfolding of the human being.

> Man is essentially reason (*Vernunft*); the man, the child, the educated and the uneducated man, all are reason, or rather the possibility of being reason is present in and given to everyone. . . . The only difference is that in the child reason is only potentially or implicitly present, while in the adult it is explicit, transformed (*gesetzt*) from possibility into existence. (1987: 74; 1940: 104)[6]

However, reason's cycle of self-development is interrupted by the fact that 'development' is concrete as the 'I' or as subjectivity. What the seed does naturally reason must do consciously. A development that knows of itself is an education that disrupts this development. It is a development that opposes development. In the sense referred to above, this opposition is what drives *Bildung*. It is the experience that re-forms what is experienced, and negates therefore the initial formation. We can say here that *Bildung* is education regarding the cycle of *Entwicklung*. *Bildung* disrupts the smooth flow of potentiality to actuality. What is actual here is the experience of the negation of development, or its being re-formed in its being known. This opposition is the history of philosophy, that is, the history of philosophy is the history of a development whose unfolding appears to exceed itself at every turn. The history of philosophy is therefore set a different and unique challenge: to comprehend a development whose comprehension obstructs development. Or, to comprehend how the I can be *of* unfolding yet also *as* unfolding. This requires a notion of education or development that, in appearing to exceed development, in fact practises development.

Between them, *Bildung* and *Entwicklung* play out an educational drama that has philosophical implications which still remain to be acknowledged and comprehended. Therefore, we move now to the third and most important notion of education in Hegel, that of *Aufhebung*, in order to show how *Bildung* and *Entwicklung* are its constitutive but not its exhaustive moments. What they constitute is the disruption of the consciousness that does not think philosophically, and the historical, theological and political *telos* of doing so. Disruption as teleology, and teleology as disruption are the motor force of Hegel's *Phenomenology of Spirit* and his *History of Philosophy*. Together they ensure that dogma is constantly negated and that the negation is understood as human development. Together here they have their relation comprehended as a self-(re-)formation in the *Aufhebung*.

Aufhebung (self-[re-]formation)

This is perhaps the most disputed term in all Hegelian thought. On it hangs the system itself because the *Aufhebung* is the mechanism by which negation and negation of negation realize a determinate self-(re-)formation. It is un-Hegelian to see Hegel's philosophy as based around the triadic relationship of thesis–antithesis–synthesis because such a formula suppresses the fact that in Hegel any such movement changes the consciousness that experiences it. This change is the culture, the formation and re-formation, of the consciousness. Merely to observe this development and to comment upon its apparent logic from a vantage point, or as a voyeur, is both to presuppose and to misunderstand this culture of experience, and of subjectivity. Indeed, it is to eschew precisely the education that the sequence of the terms describes. In the mind, let us say, of a critic of Hegel, this formula is interpreted as one in which the synthesis overcomes the opposition of thesis and antithesis. Equally, in the same mind, a critique of this overcoming might

be made on the grounds of the apparent imperialism of Eurocentric rationalism. Overcoming and resolving oppositions, the critic might say, is the
terror imposed by reason over all oppositions or dualisms. Such a critic may
champion the view, on the one hand, that differences should not be overcome or, on the other, that difference exceeds the illusory sovereignty of
the synthesis that reason seeks to impose. The former might be called the
pluralism of the postmodern, the latter the excess of the poststructural.

Hegel does not, however, have a philosophy based on such a simplistic
view of the overcoming or resolving of opposing dualisms. Hegel's philosophy and the notion of the *Aufhebung* within it are centred on the relations
that serve as the conditions of the possibility for the thinking of objects.
The sense of contingency found here is more radical, more penetrating
and more significant than versions of contingency that seek only to assert
relations of dependence. Such assertions are forced to presuppose the relation they wish to acknowledge. Or, put another way, the relation to the
object is always made possible by, and is contingent upon, a prior relation
to that object. This means not only that even assertions of contingency are
contingent, but also that this realization must in turn collapse under the
weight of itself, even, or especially, when it is posited as difference, as possibility, or as the impossibility of absolute thinking. We saw above this
re-formation as characteristic of *Bildung*.

This insight into philosophy as the relation of the relation does not, of
course, belong exclusively to Hegel. On the contrary, it is the insight into
the dialectic that gives form and content to Western philosophy from Plato
to Derrida. What is significant about Hegel's contribution to this debate[7] is
that his whole philosophy works not with the one relation or the other, but
within the relation of both relations; that is, within the relation to the object
and the relation to that relation. This is the educative significance of the
Aufhebung. It is, we might say here, to work within the broken middle[8] of the
natural standpoint of thought's relation to an object and the philosophical
standpoint of thought's relation to that relation. There is no overcoming
here although there is a double negation; the negation of the object in relation to consciousness and the negation of that relation in relation to
consciousness (now as its own object). Hegel's system is a detailed exploration into the implications of each relation upon the other. It is not a system
where mediation or negation are overcome, but rather one where philosophy, and, therefore, education in Hegel, are precisely the subject and
substance of those implications. As an essentially educative experience, this
broken middle cannot be resolved, for it precedes thinking as the latter's

condition of possibility. But what it can learn from this impossibility of resolution is its own truth, a truth known in and as the form and content of the contradictory and inevitable conjunction of abstraction and mediation. *Aufhebung* is this truth that lies within the relation of contingency to itself, and in the following section we will explore the structure of this educational relation as recollection.

Seen in this way, *Aufhebung* is the philosophical education that underpins the education of *Bildung* and *Entwicklung*, and, most importantly, their philosophical and educational relation to each other. My case, here, is this. *Bildung* in the *Phenomenology* prioritizes the reform of the thinker that comes with thought's negation of its object. *Entwicklung* in the *History of Philosophy* prioritizes the *telos* of such changes. As such, as we saw above, their relation to each other is anything but harmonious. *Telos* is already disrupted in *Bildung*, and *Bildung* always returns to (this disrupted) *telos*. It is this difficult relation – an aporetic relation – that is expressed as self-(re-)formation in and by *Aufhebung*.

Recollection

A thought has escaped: I was trying to write it down: instead I write that it has escaped me

(Pascal, 1966: 218)

Aufhebung is significant in Hegel because it achieves something that appears to the abstract rational consciousness to be impossible. It is able to know something as both an appearance and as the negation of this appearance. This means that it somehow preserves what it knows as both what it was (its appearance) and what it is now known as. When *Aufhebung* is translated as 'sublation' it fails to pay due attention to the most important feature of the *Aufhebung*, that it is essentially a learning experience. But if this was all there was to it, the *Aufhebung* would amount to no more than a sceptical knowing, that is, a knowing of things to be not as they appear. What seems to be lacking in *Aufhebung* seen in this way is any kind of positive knowledge about what the thing *actually* is. The nature of the positive element of the *Aufhebung* is what is most at stake in Hegel. If it is purely positive then it is easily fashioned into the kind of claims for absolute knowing that appear arrogant and self-satisfied. If it is not positive at all, then it teaches us nothing. What kind of notion remains, then, if any, that might somehow know the truth of something in what it is not, and maintain that negativity even in its being known as such? How might it be possible to *know* something that is known as unknown? The answer to this question, and the structure of the *Aufhebung* in Hegel, is of education as recollection. When the negative knows itself it is as recollection.

We saw in Chapter 1 how life can know its own nothingness in death, how the master can know his own nothingness in the slave, and how the self can know his nothingness in his other. But if we now replace 'know' here with 'recollect,' the educational character and structure of this knowing can be brought to the fore. To recollect oneself is to be what one is not. There is a double significance here, and one that was also found in Chapter 1 regarding life, the master and the self. First, one recollects that one is something other than what one is. This is the same as saying that one is never what one was, because the knowledge of what one was can only be recollected. It can only be known differently to how it was. This opens up a fear of only ever being nothing, a fear of nihilism, because a positive standpoint is forever impossible. But, and second, to recollect is to *be* what one is not. This is a result, albeit one that looks strange and out of sorts with rationalism. There is only one way that this opposition or autoimmunity can make sense of itself without the aid of further external presuppositions or assertions. One can *be* what one is *not* when one is learning about oneself. The structure of this learning is recollection, for in recollection what is recalled is what was by that which *is* what one was. What is lost and kept is that which is recollected as recollecting. In this learning, in this education, the positive and the negative carry their own truths at the same time in and as learning. This is how the *Aufhebung* works, through recollection, as our philosophical education that what was and what is are both present and absent in and as learning. Learning holds thought and being together without suppressing their difference. This, indeed, is what is educational about philosophy and philosophical about education.

Later in this chapter we will see how the history of philosophy appears when viewed philosophically as recollection. This is undertaken by looking at the aporetic mastery of the West and its export of vulnerability across the world. Before that, however, we will illustrate this concept of recollection, and therefore *Aufhebung*, in three ways. First, by looking at the role it plays in Hegel's presentation of the psychology of thought; second, and with the non-specialist in Hegel in mind, by way of William Wordsworth's ode 'Intimation of Immortality from Recollections of Early Childhood'; and third, albeit briefly, by looking at recollection in Philip Verene's book *Hegel's Recollection*.

Psychology

For those who seek an obvious justification from Hegel that the *Aufhebung* is recollection there is not much to go on. But what there is, goes a long way. Recollection is primarily described as a moment in the development of thought to rational cognition. In both the *Philosophical Propaedeutic* (1809–1811) and the *Philosophy of Mind* (1830) *Erinnerung* is the first stage wherein immediate intuitions come to be held as images in the memory such that they become representations. The translation of *Erinnerung* as inwardizing[9] refers to what happens when the ego or the I recollects itself from its feelings and intuitions as a presence or a being in time and space. Recollection works here by creating the intuition as an image within the ego. To know the image as mine is to know the I to whom it belongs.

But the term inwardizing does not capture the unique features of what takes place here. In the *Philosophical Propaedeutic* Hegel notes that the I does not restrict itself to the intuition that has been internalized, but also liberates this intuition from an external time and space to a subjective time and space. In this way, it is universalized as form and 'through the sublation (*das Aufheben*) of the particular time of intuition it becomes enduring (*dauerned*)' (1986: 152; 1970: 45). The nature of this universality is 'just as much a non-existent as a preserved existence' (1986: 152; 1970: 45), and it is the *Aufhebung* that preserves what is not, or what is negated. It is as recollection, then, that the I here learns to know itself in this activity as the I. The point that must not be missed is that the imagination and the I can only know of themselves as recollection through *another* recollection. This same structure is therefore repeated when thought, having itself or this I as its own object, knows itself in self-opposition. Here, the *Aufhebung* is a recollection of what the I is not as what nevertheless *is*.

As we saw above in the quotation from the final paragraph of the *Phenomenology*, recollection is not restricted to its part in the psychology of the knowing mind. In the philosophical mind recollection recalls itself and plays out the negation of the negation as formative self-determination. This is true of all mediations, not just those in the imagination, for it is how the I will know itself as recollected even within the imagination. In the latter the I recollects itself in the negation that is representation. This is true also of the recollection that is absolute spirit. In both cases there is the relation of the external in the internal, *and* the relation to that relation. The latter is the recollection of the former as itself prior to this education. This is as true for immediate intuition as it is for all representations of objects, and of the relation to these representations. Recollection is what makes the relation a triadic self-(re-)formation. This is why, also, it is the substance of spirit. This relation of the mind to the object is the fundamental relation in the whole of Hegel's philosophy. *How* it is interpreted depends on the way that recollection is posited within different social and political relations. It is when the I becomes aware of itself as that which existed without this awareness that we find the significance of recollection as philosophical education.

One way to illustrate the importance of recollection in Hegel beyond the imagination is in the way that the absolute or God can be known. In the *Philosophy of Mind* Hegel distinguishes between mere knowing (*Wissen*) and cognition (*Erkennen*). Consciousness is always an awareness of being, and as we saw, this is implicitly a recollection, but the mind also wants to know its truth. In this activity *Geist* will recollect the implicit recollection that is the I as not-I. A double recollection such as this is a double negation. The first recollection (the simple I) is recalled as negative and known as not known by a second recollection. This second recollection pulls the ground out from under its own feet in doing so. That which recollects itself as recollection loses itself to itself. Recollection here is essentially groundless. This is the same groundlessness that is feared by Aristotle and his mediaeval commentators as the *reductio ad absurdum*.[10] Hegel sees that in philosophy this groundlessness is treated only negatively, that is, as making impossible the comprehension of God. Theology, he says, will accept that we can know that God is but not what God is.[11] This says no more than that theology refuses God as recollection because the negation of the negation is seen to hold no educational and philosophical substance. Yet it is in and as education that groundlessness has its own substance. This means that we can know that God is, but also we can learn what God is. This serves as an example of how recollection underpins the movement and development that form the Hegelian system. Recollection is how immediacy is known as lost, and how mediation knows this loss as itself. This is the characteristic of all intellectual movement in Hegel that knows itself negatively, from the simple I in imagination to the absolute in cognition.

Recollection in Wordsworth

In Wordsworth's poem 'Intimation of Immortality from Recollections of Early Childhood' he describes the truth of a child and his development to the adult in terms of recollection. The child in the poem, at first, is at one with nature and the eternal universe, 'a time when meadow, grove, and stream/ The earth and every common sight,/To me did seem/Apparelled in celestial light.' But this blissful state is known to the poet only as recollection, for 'it is not now as it has been of yore;-/ Turn wheresoe'er I may,/ By night or day,/ The things which I have seen I now can see no more.' This loss of the 'child of joy' sees 'Shades of the prison-house begin to close/ Upon the growing boy.' The child is emerging into the adult world and education is doing all it can to ensure that the child is lost to the *amour-propre* of social convention, so that 'the little actor cons another part.'

Yet Wordsworth is not just drawing attention to childhood as paradise lost. Nor, indeed, is he describing the unfolding or the development of the child to the adult merely as a seed becoming a plant or as a matter merely of the passage of time. He is adding to the teleological development of the child a range of negative and contradictory experiences that by their very nature disrupt any teleology. Adult recollection has to instigate a change in the adult, to re-form his understanding of himself. If this is an inevitable part of his development then the change brought about in recollection was always its potentiality. Here one might argue that *Entwicklung* and *Bildung* are reconciled, in that the re-form of recollection was always part of the teleology, and the telos of *Entwicklung* realizes itself in *Bildung*, in the reformative experiences of recollection. But there is no such reconciliation to be had in recollection. This is because what *Entwicklung* and *Bildung* produce is the paradox of recollection, a dialectic of enlightenment where *telos* includes within it its own loss of itself to itself, and where *Bildung* is the experience of this re-formation of *telos* and therefore of the child. It is in the philosophical import of this aporetic relationship between development and reformation that we find the all-important notion of *Aufhebung*. It is found too in Wordsworth's poem. Recollection has so re-formed the adult that he cannot be the child, nor can he be as the child. The negative paradox here in recollection is that the comprehension of the child can never belong to the child. By definition the child must be re-formed as adult in order to understand the truth of the child. This paradox is summed up by Wordsworth at the very beginning of the poem saying 'the child is the father of the man', meaning the child gives birth (in recollection) to the man who is the father.[12]

How, then, does Wordsworth view this philosophical education? Recollection knows the loss of childhood in order to comprehend childhood, and it is from within the prison-house that the writer looks back at his lost childhood. But this is not nostalgia. The adult, gazing back at childhood, states that it is not for the simple delights and liberties of childhood that he gives thanks. 'Not for these I raise/ The song of thanks and praise;/ But for those obstinate questionings of sense and outward things.' And he concludes

> What though the radiance that was once so bright
> Be now for ever taken from my sight,

> Though nothing can bring back the hour
> Of splendour in the grass, of glory in the flower;
> We will grieve not, rather find
> Strength in what remains behind,
> In the primal sympathy
> Which having been must ever be,
> In the soothing thoughts that spring
> Out of human suffering,
> In the faith that looks through death
> In years that bring the philosophic mind.

Famously, it is this philosophic mind, the mind of recollection, in which 'the meanest flower that blows can give/Thoughts that do often lie too deep for tears.'[13]

What is it, then, that brings Wordsworth to claim that recollection brings even more joy than childhood itself? It is the comprehension that, in the negativity and loss contained in recollection, there is realized something of even greater significance. In Wordsworth's ode, the doubts that come with the loss of childhood are themselves formative and, because they are not overcome, continually re-formative of the adult. Doubts hold more joy, more difficulty, more depth, than can ever rest in innocence. Transposing Hegelian terms into the ode, we see that the seed of reason (the child) develops as it must from its potentiality to its actuality. But to realize this actuality reason must become self-conscious, and in doing so, reason is re-formed in a relation to itself. In knowing itself it must also lose itself. Here, the *Entwicklung* of reason is re-formed in its *Bildung.* The philosophic mind that knows of development and its negativity is reason become spirit. But neither *Bildung* nor *Entwicklung* are adequate to express the educational nature of spirit even though they are constitutive moments in it. It is *Aufhebung* that describes this educational nature of spirit.

Metaphor

Philip Verene's study of recollection in Hegel is rare in that it seeks the essence of Hegel's philosophy in education in general and in recollection in particular. In short, he argues that the key to understanding the dialectical movements of the *Phenomenology* lies in the difference between the in-itself and the in-itself that is also for-itself.[14] This, states Verene, must not be seen as a relation for to do so is to posit a third (*Dritte*) that unifies them. For Verene, these two moments – we might call them thought and the thought of this thought – are not a relation but are the condition of the possibility of relation. This '*doubled Ansich*' (1985: 16) is experience, and is 'process-like in that it is just the movement between the two moments of in itself and for itself' (1985: 108). Verene is absolutely clear here that the twoness of the *Ansich* 'can never be compressed into a oneness' (1985: 107). Instead, recollection is the way to understand and to see through the appearance of such unity. Recollection can hold the doubled *Ansich* in metaphor and image without unifying them. As such, metaphor is both a remembering of the twoness and, in its re-presentation in a new form, is 'self-altering' (1985: 20). The duality that cannot be a unity is suspended by a metaphor or an image that re-presents what cannot be expressed in a proposition. Indeed, it is what makes consciousness possible at all. The concept (*Begriff*) is always 'in friendly opposition to the image (*Bild*)' (1985: 13) because the image is what makes consciousness of itself possible.

The attraction of Verene's thesis is that it finds education at the core of Hegelian philosophy. Consciousness recollects itself in images and metaphors that allow it to express itself without filling the gap that has produced it. In this way Verene presents a Hegel that is open and non-dogmatic, one where each new recollection overturns the previous one, and where gradually the illusions and appearances of these images become known for what they are. This is the education of consciousness in the *Phenomenology* through its own experience of its misrecognitions of itself.

Verene maintains this open and non-dogmatic character in his reading of absolute knowing. Referring to the final paragraph of the *Phenomenology* (which we paraphrased near the beginning of this chapter) and particularly to the reference there to the Calvary of spirit, he argues that

> absolute spirit hangs on a cross because the annulment of time cannot be perfectly accomplished. Spirit does not create its own perfect likeness. Its friendship with its own forms is not complete. They foam out to it and it must recollect them. Experience cannot be perfectly recollected. (1985: 112)

This has implications for the relation (the metaphor?) between the *Phenomenology* and the *Science of Logic*. Here he says

> absolute knowing freely releases itself into the world of metaphysical thought, not because it has attained a unity between the two moments within the being of the subject, but because it has overcome all illusion that there is such a phenomenon. It takes up the quest for unity in

different terms; it attempts to think the 'and' of its two moments as a unity (1985: 117),

an attempt that circles back to nature and immediacy.

Such a summary does not do justice to this clear and incisive reading of Hegel's philosophy as essentially educational. However, among several differences between our two accounts of recollection, one must be mentioned here. In Verene's recollection I believe that the actuality of the absolute is sacrificed for the perceived openness of metaphor. When the in-itself becomes known for-itself this is a negation, and this can be represented metaphorically and in imagination. The continual renewal of metaphor is what ensures recollection is open and non-dogmatic. As he says, 'in the recollective act we are the image' (1985: 113). The problem here in comparison to the notion of recollection that I am employing as education in Hegel is that Verene's notion of recollection remains fixed in the imagination. Put differently, political externality remains suppressed within and by the priority given here to the inner. This amounts to a serious misrecognition of the nature of recollection. The representation of the gap in the double *Ansich* is only a single negation. But the philosophical and political import of recollection is in its double negation. It is here that the political import of recollection as actuality is to be found.

It is in the nature of recollection to know that everything that is not recollected is posited, as it is to know also that recollection is the only way positing can be known. Verene's notion of recollection does not recognize this about itself. Indeed, his notion of recollection is itself a positing that the double *Ansich* cannot be a relation. This, in turn, is to fail to recollect how the relation of the 'and' that Verene says is unknowable is already an actual political fact. This is what recollection does. It reminds us that reality is always a presupposition, but one that can only be known negatively, or as actual. In Verene's example, the relation between thought and its object that he says cannot be a relation is only the illusion of the real, the illusion that truth cannot be thought because relation would, in his view, overcome the truth of the gap. But recollected, this illusion is known as posited, and this is a critique of the posited identity of the mind that so posits. It is a critique of what consciousness failed to recollect in itself, that it is already what is (now) recollected as the political fact of presupposition.

In short, then, Verene's notion of recollection concerns only the single negation that is inwardized as image and known as the I. These are the images, as he says, of the master and the slave, the unhappy consciousness, the spiritual animal kingdom and the beautiful soul. But this is only half of their story. Verene's notion of recollection is spared its additional political implications in knowing the image as actual social relations, actual relations of political power. It does not go on to work with the double negation, the recollection of recollection, in which the image is itself recollected as a political fact. In contrast, in education in Hegel recalled reality is what is actual, and what is actual is learned as the unavoidable positing of the real as a pre-determining political fact. Actuality is essentially a political education in the recollection of the real as not known, but, and in the very nature of recognition, it is always too late to avoid this presupposition. Education in Hegel knows this complicity as its own actuality, its own education, and its own *Aufhebung*.

As a final note, Verene might respond by pointing out that he attends this double negation in absolute knowing, and in particular in the transition from the *Phenomenology* to the *Science of Logic*. He argues here that whereas all previous shapes in the *Phenomenology* had lived in the illusion that the key had to be found to uniting the double *Ansich*, now, in absolute knowing, there is the wisdom that 'the "and" is real' (1985: 116). He describes the 'real' as the space between the in-itself and the for-itself that is 'the root of the absolute liberation of consciousness, its ground of its freedom' (1985: 116) and 'represents' (1985: 116) their 'mutual attachment' (1985: 116) to each other, this time as a categoreal representation rather than a metaphorical one. It is not clear to me what Verene means by the 'real' here. If it means that the space is absolutely open then this reads the political out of absolute knowing completely, for it only makes illusion absolute. If on the other hand it means to say that the gap is now actual mutual attachment, this is only an imaginary political world. Both of these are themselves grounded in the prior positing of the absence of actuality as the third partner in the double *Ansich*. But education in Hegel teaches that the third partner is not optional. It is what recollection recollects. In addition to the single negation of Verene's notion of recollection we have to work with the double negation in which recollection knows reality actually, and knows the gap that Verene works so hard to keep open as also always already closed. This is not a metaphorical education, it is actual political life.

Cultural imperialism

Exploring the different notions of education in Hegel, and in particular how the *Aufhebung* is to be seen as recollection, now offers a way into some of the political questions that surround Hegel's history of philosophy.

I want, in particular, to think about how education in Hegel challenges the stereotype of Hegel referred to at the beginning of this chapter – the one associated with a history of philosophy that in effect seems to end history – and how it re-forms this interpretation of his concept of freedom. I will argue, now, that in thinking about the issue of Western domination in the world, *Aufhebung* and education in the history of philosophy offer a reforming of and an education about present Western mastery and freedom. *Aufhebung* as it were opens up Hegelian critique as a present history of philosophy. It is in this sense that Hegel says in the shorter *Logic*, 'the history of philosophy, in its true meaning, deals not with a past, but with an eternal and veritable present' (1975: 126).

Hegel's notion of the beginning of the history of philosophy immediately raises concerns for the perspectives in the world that are passed over as having not yet begun the pathway of despair of reason's education. Yet Hegel's beginning the history of philosophy in Ancient Athens comes about by means of philosophy as recollection. What it recollects is its own development. It looks for the potential of which it is the actuality. Its beginning, then, *is not optional*, it is pre-determined by its development to the point of this recollection. Equally, however, this undermines the standpoint of the history of philosophy *per se*, because recollection is always the groundlessness of such a standpoint. Recollection is what exposes the history of philosophy to be other than itself.

Nevertheless, there are implications here for the way Eastern traditions are categorized philosophically when freedom recollects its beginning in Ancient Athens. In the East, says Hegel, the person remains dominated by substance to the extent that consciousness is extinguished and the subject annihilated. Thus 'political freedom, law, free ethical life, pure consciousness, thinking – all these are absent. What is required for their emergence is that the subject shall set himself as consciousness over against substance and so gain recognition of himself there' (1987: 167). In sum, for the history of philosophy to begin, substance must be made a concrete objectivity, a concrete universality, so that this relation to subjectivity, at first external and alien, can bring into being the formative *Aufhebung* or education wherein the relation of subject to substance determines itself in and as freedom. Importantly here Hegel uses the figures of the master and the servant (*Herr und Knechtes*) to illustrate the fate of the will with regard to alien substance. Where the will is not universal, and where substance therefore is dominant over subject, 'there is only the status of the lord and the status of servant. This is the sphere of despotism' (1987: 169) and in it the feeling of finitude is fear. This is the case for master and servant. The latter stands in

fear and lacks in any legal recognition that might offer some form of independence. The former rules by fear, but he still lacks a recognition in
anything other than fear. Thus says Hegel, 'both are on the same level. The
difference between them is only the formal one of more or less force or
energy of will' (1987: 169). Fear, therefore, whether in the finite caprice
of the master or the finite domination of the servant was, for Hegel, 'the
ruling category of the East' (1987: 169). It follows, then, that there could be
'no philosophical knowledge in the East' (1987: 171) by which a history of
philosophy could have begun, for what was required was the recollection of
the experience of fear as self-development. In the master/servant relationship in the *Phenomenology of Spirit* and in the *History of Philosophy* what was
required for the beginning of philosophy, of wisdom, was that fear be experienced as absolute negativity, *and* known now as the self-determination of
substance. Politically, when substance is known as having this negative character then there is reason, spirit and the concept. Only when fear is formative
of the universal in the finite, a formation that is a self-determination of substance in the subject, does freedom begin to emerge. We will return to what
this means for the relation of East and West in a moment.

Much criticism is made of Hegel's Western logocentric and imperialist
'standpoint'. As we saw above, Philip Kain has recently argued for a reading
of Hegel as a cultural relativist. By this he means that the absolute should be
seen as a cultural paradigm that will shift when those it marginalizes or
excludes will come to subvert it. The other to the absolute is therefore the
critical factor in the paradigm shift. This enables Kain to claim that one can
keep the absolute in Hegel as the structure within which culture is ordered
without holding to the absolute as a closed and fixed content. But his case
rests on suppressing the educational import of the *Aufhebung* – which plays
no part in his argument – a suppression that itself rests upon ignoring the
illusory being of the reflective mind that has the absolute as its object. Without the *Aufhebung* and illusory being the contingency that Kain argues for, a
cultural contingency, never meets itself as object in a second contingency,
that is, the philosophical contingency of the culture of contingency itself. As
such, his standpoint is one that does not acknowledge the third partner in
the relation of self and other, or does not acknowledge education in
Hegel.

A different response to this has been made by the Hegel scholar Henry
Harris. He has commented that Hegel's philosophy of history, and by implication his history of philosophy, is unfortunately imbued with 'the nascent
cultural and economic imperialism of Western Europe' (1995: 5) that was

prevalent in Hegel's time. They present world history in a way that is both 'superstitious and reactionary' (1995: 5). For example, Hegel

> not only presents world history as the movement of 'Providence' (as if a superhuman agent were really involved), but also employs the myth of a 'March of the Spirit' from the Sunrise towards the Sunset to support a 'substantial' interpretation of the great Asian cultures as logically primitive. (1995: 5)

Such a view, says Harris, we now know to be 'an unhistorical fiction' (1995: 5). Harris is certain that Hegel would no longer hold to a view of the history of philosophy as simply a progressive philosophy of history that dismissed non-Christian religions in the way that he did. What Harris argues for instead is that Hegelian science be kept separate from its religious extensions. The latter are, as it were, merely cultural representations of a particular time and place. The conceptuality of science must therefore be kept apart from some of its historically contingent baggage.

To this end Harris rigorously separates the *Science of Logic* and the *Phenomenology* from any religious excesses. He describes the process of the phenomenology of spirit in the following way:

> The Gospel had to be proclaimed and Platonically interpreted in an imaginative mode; the subjective consciousness had to advance gradually from imagination to conceptual thinking. Through this historical development, human self-consciousness finally arrives at comprehension of the 'whole' within which it begins as consciousness. (1995: 94)

He concludes that it is the *Phenomenology* that is Hegel's real philosophy of world history and it is the *Phenomenology* that has eternal significance beyond the way Hegel's own time is included in ways that distort it. He mentions that at the end of the *Phenomenology* Hegel makes what Harris calls 'a puzzling comment' (1995: 95) about a commensurability between the phenomenological shapes of experience and the structure of the *Science of Logic*. Harris says that Hegel mentioned this again only once, in his Berlin lectures, and 'probably he abandoned the idea' (1995: 95). If the *Science of Logic* is historical then, says Harris, it is not 'strictly conceptual' (1995: 95). Far from being the comprehension of its own time, Harris argues that the *Logic* is the comprehension of eternity, 'the thought of God before the Creation' (1995: 100). The *Phenomenology* however 'is neither the comprehension of its own time nor the comprehension of eternity, but the universal comprehension of time as such' (1995: 100). Thus, its lessons are not bound to their time in the way that Hegel's 'real' philosophy is, and by 'real' here Harris means the real experiences of the system within their own historical context. The distinction here is that 'phenomenology moves away from actual experience towards pure logic; the System moves from pure Logic back to real experience' (1995: 98) as and in nature and spirit. Harris mentions here the views prevalent in Hegel's time on the state, war, punishment, science and technology. These are specific to real philosophy, but not to understanding the ladder of the *Phenomenology* to pure logic. What was present to Hegel as objective and real has become for us something known phenomenologically, that is, as part of the appearances that educate us to science. We are still charged with having 'to achieve the comprehension of our own time for ourselves' (1995: 97). This means, says Harris, that the more Hegel's real philosophy becomes for us a historical curiosity, the more we will comprehend the relevance of his logic to our own situation.

However, and in response to this view in Harris, it can be said that his separation of logic from culture can be seen also as cultural and as a stage of religious representation. To refuse this present complicity of pure logic with cultural spirit risks being as superstitious and reactionary as he accuses Hegel of being about his own time. What is at stake in Harris's interpretation is the question of complicity in the mastery of the West's view of itself in relation to its non-Western others. We will explore this in a moment. But regarding Harris we must raise again the question, is it not just another cultural reproduction to be separating logic from culture? Hegel's comment seen above regarding the commensurability of the phenomenological stages of experience and the structure of the *Science of Logic* – a comment that Harris is happy to dismiss – in fact goes to the heart of the matter regarding Western logocentric domination. There has to be a commensurability here because the *Logic* is also a phenomenological shape of experience. The beginning that is not a beginning in Being is its positing of itself. This positing parades as essence or the reflective mind, but it is merely illusory being (*Schein*). This illusion then continues to learn how philosophically it is substantial and a real philosophical experience. Absolute knowing, therefore, repeats the structure of the master/servant relationship, that is, of itself constituted in and by its determination in independence *and* dependence, and in life *and* death. Real modern social relations triumph in the *Logic* because absolute knowing is returned to the question of method, which is precisely where the *Logic* began, that is, with the question of its own beginning.[15] The *Logic* may be called pure culture in the sense that the oppositions of *Bildung* have become their own content, and thus become absolute knowing because recollection is known philosophically as *Aufhe-bung*, as thought's own self-determination. *But* to separate logic from culture altogether where 'there is no interaction with historical experience' (1995: 95) is to repeat a standpoint of natural (Western) law, in Harris's case, the standpoint of the appearance of pure thinking. He may be right to say that in the climax to the *Logic* 'the last vestige of the traditional concept of God has vanished' (1995: 103), but this is not the same as saying that experience 'is left behind' (1995: 93).

The illusion, here, is that the standpoint that criticizes Hegel for his nascent cultural imperialisms is not itself also just such a nascent cultural imperialism. The critique in Harris of Hegel's Western mastery is another mastery. Failure to recognize this mastery is one of spirit's most important modern shapes. A more philosophical Hegelian critique is to recognize that cultural imperialism is already present, and inescapable, in the critique of imperialism. What this looks like I want to explore briefly in the following section. But let me be clear here. I am not trying to argue that Harris is somehow arguing for a completion of experience. He is clear, as we saw, that we must comprehend our own time for ourselves, and that this will be helped the more that Hegel's own time appears as a historical curiosity. I am not arguing that Harris is arguing for an ahistorical science. Rather, I am making the point that his argument for present science risks becoming ahistorical when he criticizes Hegel for cultural baggage without, also, recognizing the logic of this critique in its own political actuality.

The standpoint of mastery

At stake here is the complicity of critique in the relations it critiques. It is a complicity that is accompanied by a mastery, even if an unwitting one, because the power lies in the conditions of the possibility of critique. The mastery is in the posited standpoint of the critique of imperialism. A genuinely speculative critique has to contain its mastery and the collapse of its standpoint in the contingency of contingency that underpins its groundless and absolute determination.

As such, in this final section of this chapter we will bring this education in Hegel found in the history of philosophy to bear on the present standpoint of Western mastery. Thus far, this chapter has presented a view of the history of philosophy as more than merely a justification of sovereignty by the Western master. It has argued, in particular, for an educative relationship between development, culture and the *Aufhebung* that re-forms any such attempts at justification. The perspective that recollects itself in the history of philosophy disrupts any merely linear pattern of development. This has been expressed above in the recognition that the history of philosophy is by definition held hostage by that which the history of philosophy itself makes possible. This has implications for the epistemological status of the history of philosophy. Any claim made for a commensurablility of past and present as the one development collapses in the recollection that divides them, and has its truth in the *Aufhebung* that knows (learns) this truth of recollection. As with education in Hegel in each of the chapters of this book, the *Aufhebung* here is not a simple reconciliation of spirit with its history, it is the essential openness to the lack of reconciliation, learned and re-learned, and formed and re-formed in this learning.

What, then, can this view of the recollection of the history of philosophy offer to an examination of Western mastery in relation to its others? Recollection in the history of philosophy is the same educational experience of death in life and of the other in the self that we saw in Chapter 1. What is recollected in the history of philosophy is the East in the West (and, although not our subject here, of the West in the East). This seems a remarkable claim, not least because, as we have recorded, the history of philosophy is primarily seen as the West without the East at all. But it is the truth of education in Hegel that what is learned is how the other is present in the self. In this case, then, how is the East[16] present in the standpoint of the mastery of the West? I will argue now that it is present as the export of fear and vulnerability by the West.

To make this case we must draw again on the way that Hegel uses the master and slave relation to characterize freedom in the East and in the West. In philosophical terms, where there is only fear of arbitrary power, there the relation is one of despotism. It is not until fear is itself the truth of the master that a modern notion of freedom is possible. But this modern notion of freedom does not stand apart from its pre-modern counterpart. It stands always in relation to it and this relation is determined by the relation that the master has to fear. The idea that it stands apart and separate from the pre-modern is precisely the shape the modern mastery takes when it misrecognizes its own relation to fear and vulnerability. They are both – the pre-modern and the modern – shapes of the life and death struggle as the actual relation of master and slave and self and other. This means that the criticisms made of the way the history of philosophy eschews the East misunderstand the shapes of the relation of East and West that the history of philosophy learns in recollection. Any claims that the East is overlooked, or even more controversially, that it should not be represented philosophically as fear without freedom, hides two crucial things. First, they take the West to be the yardstick of what is and is not to be deemed as freedom. Second, in doing so, they perpetuate the illusion that the West is independent from fear. They fail, in other words, to recollect the relation of West and East, of freedom and fear, and fail to recognize how the West relates to fear in its modern freedoms. Education in Hegel can retrieve this relation and with it the truth of the way the East is in the West.

Hegel is clear about the formative actuality of fear and vulnerability. Both in the *Lectures on the History of Philosophy* and most famously in the master/ slave section of the *Phenomenology*, he quotes Ps. 111.10 – 'The fear of the Lord is the beginning of wisdom'.[17] The ambiguity here is instructive. The 'of' in fear of the Lord can and does mean two things at once. It refers to the fear that the servant has of the master and to the fear that the master has of his own finitude, the very thing in which originates his need to rule over others. Freedom is wholly dependent upon fear because freedom is determined by the relation to fear. In the life and death struggle life has fear as other. In the master and slave relation the master has fear as other. And in modernity the property owning person has fear as other. In each case, life, the master, and the modern person have their sovereignty grounded in their freedom from fear. They have exported fear to that which is not them, that is, to that which is other. It is wrong therefore to pit East against West, fear against freedom, as if only the former in each pairing has social relations based in the master and slave relation. In the West this relation is actual as the illusion that there is no slave, that the person who owns property need no longer fear for his sovereignty. In fact, what has happened here is that fear has been pushed away, out of sight so that it is out of mind. Freedom from fear is the illusion of Western sovereignty.

This illusory freedom is achieved in the ways that the West has found to export its fear to those who are its others – and remember here that the definition of the 'other' is part of the freedom of the master. Fear and vulnerability are exported to the poor of the world as part of the freedom to enjoy affordable possession of goods and resources. They are exported as capital, as trade, as war, and even as charity and aid. Cruelly, perhaps, in these last examples, even when the West tries to embrace vulnerability it finds it to be autoimmune.

Seen in this way the East is present in the West. What differs is that the West enjoys the illusion that the East is not present. East and West are the one truth of self and other. It is precisely because they are self and other that they are not exclusive of each other, which means, in turn, that their

differences can be comprehended in ways that educate about their relation. In the East fear has freedom as other. In the West freedom has fear as
other. In education in Hegel this is the relation wherein 'I am already other
and the other is not me.' There exist many tensions in the East as freedom
makes itself known as the truth of fear. There are similar tensions in the
West as fear returns to haunt its vulnerable freedoms. Together they educate themselves and each other.

If the West was to risk this education regarding its relation to its fears and
vulnerabilities then it would risk also the re-formation of its own freedom
according to its truth. The master can learn again the truth of the slave, and
learn how to embrace the powerless as its own truth. We may not know what
such an education would look like but we know it would not leave the West,
the master, as he is now. He already re-learns universality because he knows
he fears losing it. But this fear of loss is not yet his truth in the sense that it
can determine his relation to universality. But it is a real fear because it fears
its truth so much. This fear of truth is fear of freedom's own development.

It is, then, the education of the master that the West must attend to. This,
however, is still an education that awaits the West. It would constitute a
surrender not *of* the universal but *for* the universal. It is how the West can
learn of freedom again from within the fear that guards it, and wherein this
fear can itself be the path to a re-formed notion of universality – world
spirit. This is the risk that freedom demands.

The end of the history of philosophy

A history of philosophy, then, that eschews recollection eschews therein its
own philosophical character. Such eschewal avoids acknowledging that
looking back over the history of philosophy recollects the *telos* as present
and as disrupted. A history of philosophy that avoids the implications of this
re-formation is the adult who never sees the child as his own parent. Such
an adult is in a state of denial regarding his upbringing. But a history of
philosophy that understands the paradoxes of development and re-formation understands that the history of philosophy has its condition of possibility
in recollection. Recollection unavoidably is the method of the history of
philosophy but it falls to *Aufhebung* to know the history of philosophy within
recollection, *and* to comprehend the philosophical structure of recollection as self-(re-)formation. Recollection comprehends the history of
philosophy as development, but it is the *Aufhebung* that comprehends this
recollection as development, as formative and re-formative of *Vernunft*, of

reason that is speculative. History is the development of philosophy but philosophy is the re-formation of history as development.

There is a further implication here, however, and one that re-forms the reputation of Hegel as the dogmatic philosopher *par excellence*. It is that in education as recollection Western philosophy arrives at the point of its most radical openness to itself. The truth of recollection, and of education in Hegel, lies in knowing that what is known is not known, or that it is without ground. Judged merely abstractly, such education and learning is seen as overcoming what is not known, or where knowing replaces not knowing. This is how the absolute in Hegel is taken to mean the end of the history of philosophy and indeed the end of history *per se*. But what recollection learns does not overcome its groundlessness or ignorance. It learns of itself as the truth of this groundlessness. It is the truth of knowing what is known as not known – and this sentence is deliberately ambiguous, lending itself to meaning that nothing is known and that therein nothing *is* known. This is the educational truth of subjective substance in Hegel.

This is an end of the history of Western philosophy in one sense. It is the end of the standpoint of reason that is ignorant of its own ignorance. But as such it is also the beginning of a deep educational openness wherein the Western master consciousness is for the first time able to learn of its truth in otherness, both its own and that of its others. The West has had to learn how to be open to the truth of learning. Having done so it is ready to begin learning again. What has been learned in the history of Western philosophy becomes now the struggle for openness to a future history of world spirit. This struggle of world spirit from the West's point of view will be the struggle to be open to learning how its truth is in knowing that it does not know. Or, its struggle will be to learn and re-learn that its own truth is already other and that the other is not its truth.

Perhaps the last history of Western philosophy has been or is being written. But for this to be true the last shall also be first, for the new history of (self-[re-]reforming) Western philosophy has already begun. It recollects now that its own truth without ground is a retrospective viewpoint with a future significance that re-forms the standpoint of the present. It has to be, for although the owl of Minerva flies at sunset, nevertheless the truth of its groundless flight is already its openness to the new day that it heralds.[18]

Notes

1 I will not in this chapter look at Hegel's discussion of recollection in the Ancient world or in Plato in particular. In brief, however, he argues that two types

of recollection can be found in Plato: one which is empirical, the other which is absolute. He notes that Plato turned to myth and religion in depicting the second but points out that Plato does not present this as philosophical doctrine. See Hegel 1974: 32–36; 1970: 42–46.

[2] I will return to Kain's work a little later in this chapter.

[3] I use *re-form* in this chapter to emphasize speculative movement, as opposed to *reform* which is abstracted from such movement.

[4] Whereas the Berlin Introduction of 1820 is Hegel's own manuscript, the Introductions that I draw on now are from 1823/25/27 and are taken from the notes of students attending Hegel's lectures.

[5] Clearly current environmental events teach us that this circle can be dramatically affected by reason. It remains to be seen whether nature has any defence to this.

[6] The translation of *gesetzt* here as 'transformed' obscures the nature of positing and the way that it recollects itself, and therein the role of recollection in actuality.

[7] And, I would argue, to Kant, Nietzsche and Kierkegaard; see Tubbs, 2004.

[8] This phrase was employed recently by Gillian Rose; see Rose, 1992. It refers in turn to the idea – from a letter by Adorno to Walter Benjamin – that the thought of the whole by modern reason is the experience of 'torn halves of an integral freedom, to which, however, they do not add up' (Adorno, 1999: 130). See also Chapter 3 and Tubbs, 2000.

[9] This is so, for example, in Wallace's translation of the *Philosophy of Mind*. It stands in contrast to Verene's argument, mentioned below, that the translation of *Erinnerung* as recollection loses its sense of inwardizing.

[10] Aquinas, for example, says that 'everything that is multiform, mutable and capable of defect must be reducible to a source in something that is uniform, immutable and capable of no defect' (1975a: 40).

[11] See Hegel, 1990: 190–92, para. 445, *zusatz*, and Hegel 1988: 88.

[12] Compare this speculative insight to the medieval view of Avicenna who refuses relation its own substance; 'fatherhood is not in the son . . . fatherhood is in the father. . . . There is nothing here at all which is of both of them. . . . As for a state posited for both fatherhood and sonship, this is something unknown to us and has no name' (Avicenna , 2005: 118). This, of course, has implications for the relation of God and Christ.

[13] A similar conclusion is to be found in St Augustine's *City of God*; see, Book IX, chapter 12.

[14] This is based to some extent on paragraphs 85–86 of the *Phenomenology*, the same paragraphs I refer to in the *Introduction*.

[15] I have offered a reading of the master/servant relationship in the *Science of Logic* in Tubbs, 2004, chapter 2.

[16] I have to stress here that the concept of 'the East' does not refer empirically to any particular country. 'The East' is being used here as a concept of freedom's relation to itself, as Hegel does in the history of philosophy.

[17] See also Aquinas's discussion of this Psalm in the *Summa Theologiae* (Aquinas, 1920: 229; Part II. 2nd Part. 19. 7) who, with Ecclesiasticus (1916: Book I, and Book XXV. 12) argues that although fear is appropriate in knowing God, faith is the beginning of wisdom regarding first principles and essence.

[18] See Introduction, footnote 11.

Chapter 3

Fossil Fuel Culture

Politics aimed at the formation of a reasonable and mature mankind remain under an evil spell, as long as they lack a theory that takes account of the totality that is false

(*Adorno, 1991: 28*)

Introduction

In this chapter I explore the significance of education in Hegel in relation to some of the issues about freedom, representation and philosophy that are raised by the nature of our modern fossil fuel culture. In particular I will examine education in Hegel in regard to the illusions that endure within fossil fuel culture and to their philosophical significance. I am not concerned here with the disputed causes or effects of global warming, or with predictions about when the supplies of oil will run dry.[1] My interest is rather to show how the freedoms made possible by burning fossil fuels have contributed to a culture which liberates personal freedom from the relation to the other, to death and to the universal. One implication of this, I will argue, is resignation at the unavoidability of complicity within the representation of this political totality, a resignation that is deemed wrongly to hold no further educational significance.

When I first published a version of this chapter[2] I was able to discern its origin in three elements. First, the fuel protests in the UK in September 2000 which illustrated the absolute dependency of the social upon fossil fuels. It was a strange moment as the country moved inexorably towards complete breakdown within only a few days, and equally strange how, just before meltdown, the protesters went home. The second event was the invasion of Iraq by American and coalition forces, a campaign fuelled by the relationship between freedom and oil. And third, I remember reading the following introduction to a book written by Peter McLaren, a notable critical theorist and critical pedagogue in the USA, and being struck by just how embedded fossil fuel culture is in determining the modern idea of freedom. Having revealed his despair at the possibilities for critical transformation, McLaren ends his introduction with the following:

> Living in Los Angeles is like being encysted in a surrealist hallucination. Yet as I look at the city from this café window, things don't seem that bad: Kid Frost pulsates through the airwaves; a 1964 Chevy Impala cruises the street in all its bravado lowrider beauty; the sun is shining bountifully on brown, black and white skin (albeit prematurely aging the latter); my gas tank is full and the ocean is reachable before the heat gets too heavy and the streets get too packed. I'll take Olympic Boulevard toward Venice, searching for that glimmer of light in the eyes of strangers, seeking out that fertile space to connect, picking through that rag-and-bone shop of lost memories, and seizing that splinter of hope at the fault line of the impossible where the foundation of a new public sphere can be fashioned out of the rubble of concrete dreams. (McLaren, 1997: 14)

In this revised and extended version of the article I can now call upon a fourth element. I recently attended a workshop for critical educators from across the world. Its purpose was to re-think how the language of critical education might be revised in order for it to reflect more closely the circumstances of (late) modernity. At one point, a member of the group admitting feeling guilty that, in order to attend such a forum, he had had to enlarge his own carbon footprint by flying half way across the world. It is not this confession that I take to be as significant here as the reaction of the group to the comment. His remark was met with wry smiles and chuckles from all of us who had travelled to the meeting. These were the smiles and chuckles of a collective resignation, that in order to attend such a meeting to consider the plight of the under-privileged and the oppressed, we had to contribute to environmental changes. The smiles and chuckles in effect said: You are right, but what choice do we have?

A justification for this or any such meeting might be made on the grounds that the importance of the subject under discussion merited this small increase in carbon emissions. Nobody expressed the opposite view, that the needs of the environment outweighed the need of the participants to discuss together the needs of the poor. This in itself warns of one of the most important of all barriers to reducing the carbon footprint. Everyone can justify why, for them, every trip they make is important and necessary. The bigger picture is just too far removed from these expressions of personal freedom. I will return to this theme in a moment. Even the foreign holiday can be justified in terms of the benefits it will bring the economy in terms of increased effectiveness at work. With this in mind it is doubtful, is it not, that the stage will ever be reached where we are all politically or ethically accountable for our carbon footprints, or that we have to make a case in writing to the guardians as to why our journey is absolutely necessary. For one thing – and I will argue this case in a moment – this is unlikely because it offends directly and unambiguously our modern sense of personal freedom.

However, what I want to pick up here in the smiles and chuckles of the participants is what it reveals about attitudes towards both paradox and complicity. The paradox was recognized by all at some level that saving the world on the one hand meant contributing to its pollution on the other. The struggle requires such complicity. There is no way to avoid it. I want to draw out two things here. First, such a reaction signals, I think, to a greater or lesser extent how complicity in paradox invokes resignation. Such a total paradox held for the participants no further education. The paradox is therefore seen as a dead end. It is essentially nothing. It highlights another aspect of this world against which, even though we struggle for change, we must admit our powerlessness. Second, however, this paradox has the potential to educate the master further regarding the nature of this totality and any resignation to it. This is where education in Hegel would begin, in the despair of the totality of our contingency within pre-determined ways of living and thinking, by asking about the political import of the despair, its determination within political conditions, and what it has to teach us about attitudes towards mastery and freedom. But, as is usual, the smiles and the chuckles at the paradox of complicity lasted only a few seconds. In resignation – not admitted to but present in each small shrug of the shoulders – the discussion moved on, moved back to saving the world. The group was able, once again, to put the paradox behind it.

I want to make an unpalatable and perhaps dangerously over-stated comparison here. Let us suppose a guard gets up one morning, breakfasts, says goodbye to his wife and children, and sets off for his day's work in Auschwitz. Let us suppose, also, that at some time during his day it occurs to him, as it well might have done before, that the work he is engaged in is harmful. Might he smile quickly to himself, chuckle, and with a small, perhaps invisible shrug of the shoulders, move on and continue his work? Might he not think, rightly, that present conditions do not allow for anything different? If he protests, or deserts, he will likely be shot. Against this cold totality what choice does he have but to continue his work? And having done so, he will, again, be able to find reason for the work he does.

Is it clear what point I am trying to make here? I am not saying that the carbon footprint of a day's academic work is comparable to the military jackboot of the guard. However, I have at least to admit that I cannot know for certain that environmental changes will not proceed from droughts and food shortages to the destruction of whole communities, whole societies, perhaps even whole races. Rather, what I am seeking to do here is to bring alongside each other the shared attitude of the academic and the officer regarding the absolute totalities of their situation. It is common, and easy, to hold the guard accountable for his actions within a situation which – who knows – he may have had little choice about. It is so often asked of the Holocaust, how could they, meaning the German people, have let it happen? This question is naïve in the extreme. The implication behind the question is this: if I had been in the same situation I would not have taken part, and I would have opposed it. Yet is it not possible, perhaps likely, that at some point in the future the same question will be asked of the West in general regarding world poverty, environmental damage, and warfare: how could they (we) have let it happen? Here the shrug of resignation at the paradox of the totality by the academic may well be put alongside the shrug of the guard. The latter has his resignation focused by the threat of his own death, and dishonour to his family. Modern Western academics usually have no such immediacy. How will they fare when history asks: how could they have let it continue? Surely they must have seen the relationship between the rich, over-fed, over-fuelled and over-indulgent West and the poor, under-fed, under-privileged and under-cast South and East? Will they shrug their shoulders at the paradox of complicity that faced them, and perhaps say, you weren't there; how could you understand? The circumstances now are different to those of the camps, but is the justification for carrying on not horribly similar, and grounded in the failure to address the totality of the paradox of complicity?

If you read the above and find there, somehow, an excuse for the actions of the guard, then you have missed the point I hoped to make. The point here is the need for an education in Hegel regarding the ambivalent nature of totality, paradox and complicity. This education offers neither the standpoint of opposition to, nor a resignation in, despair at the nature of the totality. Rather, it concerns the ways in which the freedoms that fossil fuels have made possible for us in the West have determined that totality, hiding at the same time their role in doing so. I have no doubt that the guard should have preferred his own death to that of the hundreds whose deaths he contributed to everyday. But we do not prefer our own death, or even a slight fall in our own living standards, to the death of the poor around the world every day. With an education in Hegel we can learn about our own complicity from the judgements we make about how others should have behaved differently within their own paradox of complicity. I want now, to explore this paradox of the complicity of freedom when it is politically and socially determined and developed as present fossil fuel culture.

Losing the object

Hegel's claim that 'religion and the foundation of the state are one and the same' (1984: 452) is a philosophical statement about philosophy's own conditions of possibility. Philosophy is the thinking in which consciousness represents objects, including itself, to consciousness. In this broken middle of form and content, and of thought and being, philosophy depends for its representation of itself on prevailing political configurations of the object. Philosophy is just such a political configuration. The dialectic which represents philosophy to itself is therefore always between representation and the political. The representation of the political includes the determination of representation by the political. The configuration of the political is already its representation in thought. We might say here that representation is already political, and that the political reverts to representation. The way that this dialectic is itself represented in thought as an object is its 'culture'. 'The work of culture (*Bildung*),' says Hegel, is 'the production of the Form of Universality' (Hegel, 1956: 417; 1970: 496). Not only does philosophy have 'the condition of its existence in culture (*Bildung*)' (1956: 68; 1970: 92), culture itself is the appearance of freedom, the relation of state and religion, as it is represented in consciousness. There is, here, a dialectic within a dialectic. Thought, itself a relation of state and religion, is philosophy within the culture of this relation. There are two representations here; one is of the political, the other is of the relation of representation and the political. The latter is the culture of philosophy.[3] In what follows, I want, very briefly, to explore two things: first how the culture of ideology has developed since the critiques of Horkheimer, Adorno and Benjamin; and second how this is reflected in philosophy. I will argue that the relation of representation and the object within both the culture of ideology and the culture of philosophy are currently configured as fossil fuel culture and the end of culture, respectively, and that implicit in both is an aesthetic of destruction, or fascism. I will then turn to the concept of illusory being in Hegel to illustrate the educational significance of education in Hegel regarding the paradox of complicity.

In the Hegelian-Marxist tradition of critique, fascism is the representation of unmediated consciousness. It is, therein, a culture without its representation in philosophy as culture. This 'representation' is served by the liquidation of opposition, both physical and intellectual, the imperative to conformity, the mythical superiority of race, the fetishism of ideology, and by the erasure of the universal. Adorno and Horkheimer in particular reflect upon this total domination of thinking by way of the culture industry. They note, for example, that 'the whole world is made to pass through the filter of the culture industry' (1979: 126), that the culture industry 'has moulded men as a type unfailingly reproduced in every product' (1979: 127) and that 'no independent thinking must be expected from the audience: the product prescribes every reaction' (1979: 137).

They argued that three factors in particular contribute to the dominance of conformity and resignation. First, the film determines the equivalence of the audience. Each is interchangeable with any other such that there are no others. Second, the culture industry is iatrogenic, (re)producing conditions it claims to overcome. Not only is free time highly mechanized, but even the pleasure and joy offered in free time by the culture industry have become ideological; the less they satisfy, the more they reproduce the appetite for them. Third, the aesthetic of representation has separated itself from the object such that the consumer worships the image of the event more than its reality. When no exchange is required, fetishism is released from objects and is traduced into an aesthetic representation of itself.

Put these three factors together and you have a very powerful picture of the inner workings of Fascism. Thinking, removed from its negative relation to the object, is representation become the aestheticization of the political. The bourgeois person, removed from the political recognition of being object to himself, as to other, becomes an unmediated singularity and ripe for incorporation into an aesthetic of authenticity. Fascism thrives within the separation of thought from object and of person from negation, positing these illusions of independence as mastery at the same time as refusing recognition of their determination in the relation (or in this case the non-relation) of state and religion. To the critical consciousness separation of inner and outer are 'torn halves of an integral freedom to which, however, they do not add up' (Adorno, 1999: 130). This unresolved yet disavowed dualism defines the illusory mastery of the bourgeois. Every advance of pseudo-individuality, of a posited unity between the separated parts, 'took place at the expense of the individuality in whose name it occurred, so that nothing was left but the resolve to pursue one's own particular purpose . . . at odds with himself and everyone else' (1979: 155). Such a man 'is already virtually a Nazi' (1979: 155), freed from responsibility to the other as to the universal because, through 'the miracle of integration' (1979: 154) he is all others.

Walter Benjamin arrives at similar conclusions from a very different direction. Two of his most important critiques of representation are on allegory in German Baroque *Trauerspiel* and on mechanical reproduction. Both critiques work within the dialectic of form and content, or representation and philosophy.

In his study of the *Trauerspiel* Benjamin illustrates how the relation of state and religion is represented in allegory. The Counter-Reformation saw the inward anxiety regarding salvation related to the external world deserted by God. In this 'hopelessness of the earthly condition' (Benjamin, 1985: 81) the Baroque ethic consists of an inner asceticism, the beautiful soul, and a political ruthlessness, the intriguer. One of the key elements here is the way that negation is represented in and as mythical, universal ornamentation. This representation then grants to itself emergency powers by which to restore, and repeatedly fail to restore, the universal. Allegory is not just the representation of the content of the fallen world. It is itself the form of the separation between the creaturely and the divine. As such, it is both the representation of the political and the culture of that representation. Allegory marks the aestheticization of a world without salvation where monument, ornamentation and ruin are the representation of the political, the politics of representation, and the culture of their relation. This representation, this Baroque culture, is, according to Gillian Rose, 'the spirit of fascism, or what *Fascism means*' (Rose, 1993: 196).[4] It is negation become immediate, or the aesthetic of destruction. It is, dramatically, where the I has its being as destruction. It is, says Benjamin, a 'godless spirituality, bound to the material as its counterpart, such as can only be concretely experienced through evil' (Benjamin, 1985: 230).

Benjamin's other celebrated example of the aestheticization of the political is mechanical reproduction. As the ruin of objects represented the loss of the relation to the divine, so the decay of the aura of objects represents the loss of relation to the object. Both are the aesthetic of destruction, or the spirit of Fascism. Both are the melancholia and mourning of the deserted and the violence of the politician. Both are destruction, inner and outer, enjoyed as an end in itself. As Benjamin writes, the self-alienation of mankind 'has reached such a degree that it can experience its own destruction as an aesthetic pleasure of the first order. This is the situation of politics which Fascism is rendering aesthetic' (1992: 235).

A third critique of the relation of state and religion as Fascism is provided by Rose in her essay 'Beginnings of the day: Fascism and representation' (Rose, 1996). Against the piety of those who mystify the Holocaust, who deem it ineffable and unrepresentable, Rose offers the chiasmus of the fascism of representation and the representation of Fascism. As with Adorno and Horkheimer in relation to ideology, and as with Benjamin in relation to allegory and mechanical reproduction, Rose is arguing for the insistence of the dialectic between power and its forms, and the cultural representation of this dialectic. The representation of Fascism is fascist when its own power is effaced or when its mediation between subject and object spares the audience 'the encounter with the indecency of their position' (Rose, 1996: 45). She distinguishes between the educational value of the film *Schindler's List* as informative, which it achieves, and its refusal to implicate the audience in the crisis, a crisis which it makes 'external' (1996: 47). Here, she argues, sentimentality overcomes complicity because the audience is denied the ambivalence of the 'pitiless immorality' (1996: 47) that determines the whole. Thus Schindler's dilemma becomes congratulatory and the audience views the whole from the viewpoint of 'the ultimate predator' (1996: 47) who can survey the cycle of life, or the totality of culture, as voyeur. In this case, the fascism of the representation of Fascism is not only the aestheticization of the political; it is also the law-establishing violence of this aesthetic. Its ideology and the decay of aura are implied in Rose's critique of the fascism of representation and the representation of Fascism.

Rose does not make these observations in order to illustrate the impossibility of representing the Holocaust. On the contrary, she is illustrating the persistence of the baroque spirit in modernity. The spirit of Fascism persists in the representation of Fascism and it persists in the way that it aestheticizes political/religious experience. The objectivity of negation in which the experience of the whole is commended becomes, in the fascism of the representation of Fascism, an aesthetic of Being, absolved from the agon of representation and therefore, from possible resistance. Without the dialectic of representation and culture, or power and its forms, without the 'persistence of always fallible and contestable representation [which] opens the possibility for our acknowledgement of mutual implication in the fascism of our cultural rites and rituals' (1996: 41), there is no engagement with the difficulty of universal politics. All that remains in this fallen state is the *praxis* of despair, or intrigue. The ruthless predation that carries us to the cinema is rewarded with the representation of itself, again, and we leave baptized, again, in the holy waters of voyeurism, of the decay of aura. The movie provides enjoyment because it reinforces the Baroque spirit that took us there in the first place.

How, then, can representation represent its own contestability? For Rose, '*the risk* of the *universal* interest . . . requires representation, the critique of representation, and the critique of the critique of representation' (1996: 62). For Benjamin it is the politicization of art that is required. For Adorno and Horkheimer, the self-destruction of the mythical representation of enlightenment *'must examine itself*' (1979: xv). Each of these in their own ways shows how the relation to the object in modern culture threatens distraction and destruction in the spirit of Fascism, yet also commends the re-education of the philosophical consciousness that experiences the representation of the object and the political as its own culture. They do not commend a 'restoration'. They commend the education in which the dialectic becomes its own object in and of itself as learning.

Fossil fuel culture

These three critical perspectives share the view, then, that a critique of total ideology can be sustained against its inner tendency to render critique nugatory. However, this commonality in Rose, Benjamin, and Adorno and Horkheimer can hide a significant reconfiguration of the structure of ideology which demands, now, a re-examination of the representation of the political and the politics of representation. As a contribution to this, I suggest that the absolute godless spirituality of fascist culture can be discerned in two further features of modern bourgeois society. The first appears in exploring the relationship between developments in the structure of ideology and the status, literally the reality, of the object. I will argue that, in three interrelated movements, ideology and its form as culture have re-formed our relation to the object. This re-formation moves first from the dialectic of enlightenment to the ideology of ideology[5] and then to what I will term *fossil fuel culture*. The second feature lies in the appearance of the end of culture. Culture here terminates all relations to itself, that is, all educational significance. It is in education in Hegel that the educational import of culture is retrieved. In the first of these features, which we will explore in this section, we will see the disfiguration of culture as freedom from an absent universal. In the second feature, discussed in the following section, we will see this disfiguration of culture appearing as the end of culture, 'end' here referring to the termination of the education that comes from having itself as its own object. Implicit in both is a concept of freedom which embodies an aesthetic of destruction. The symbol of a death's head cited by Benjamin as 'the heart of the allegorical way of seeing' (1985: 166) lives on in both the bourgeois conception of freedom and in its representation in thought.

The dialectic of enlightenment stands as a critique of the form and content of bourgeois ideology. It revealed the abstraction of the object from its process of production in thought and the fetishism of this knowledge of abstraction. It sought no absolution from this totality of the reproduction of fetishism in thought for there was, of course, no form of theory that could withstand the market place. Critique collaborated in the conditions of the possibility of its object. As such, the dialectic of enlightenment included within its own contradictory logic the fetishism of the object, the critique of this fetishism and the critique of the critique of fetishism, the latter marking the recognition of the return of enlightenment to myth. The point of continuing to implicate critique in this way was, as Adorno and Horkheimer remarked in *Dialectic of Enlightenment*, that the enlighten-ment must continue to examine itself. The culture of ideology, its representation of the universal, the critique of that representation, and the critique of that critique could still be known *as* culture. As such, culture continued to commend itself as the impossibility and possibility of the cri-tique of ideology. Culture, as contradiction, still carried political significance; its phenomenology, its being experienced, was the representation of the political and the politics of that representation. In reproducing bourgeois social relations the culture of the dialectic of enlightenment retained a notion of the universal, of totality, in and as culture and as such retained the import of culture as our philosophical education.

The stakes regarding the critique of ideology were raised again in Adorno's formulation of ideology as image and reality in his specific critique of the culture industry. The sophistication of his analysis is not found in the vulgar idea that the culture industry merely socializes consciousness. Culture as industry, or mass objectification, is not best read within a model of base and superstructure. The latter is itself an example of the effacing of its own implication within the totality, and, in turn, is a reduction of culture to bifurcation without immanent or philosophical significance. Rather, the political significance of Adorno's critique of the culture industry lies in its modification of the dialectic of enlightenment. We noted above Adorno's observation that exchange value, the 'social' relation between fetishized objects, was no longer tied to objects of exchange. The freedom of the image from the object means, as we saw, that the ticket to the game is worshipped more than the game 'itself'. In his critique of the culture industry Adorno extended the scope of this observation. The fact that reality is separated even from its appearance as an object means that this fetishism, as reality, can be mechanically reproduced in many different ways. The result is that in and through cultural reproduction, reality – already an image – becomes the image of itself, or what Adorno calls the 'ideology of ideology' (1991: 159). Thus says Adorno, 'reality becomes its own ideology through the spell cast by its faithful duplication' (1991: 55) and 'image on the other hand turns into immediate reality' (1991: 55). In a mode of social relation which is central to the persistence of the baroque spirit in modernity, reality is already image and image is already reality. Note here that image does not 'revert' to reality as in the formulation of the dialectic of enlightenment. This change marks the development in the form of bourgeois ideology. It has effaced from its structure any trace of dialectic. Here reality and image are the one immediate (non) relation.

This marks, then, a different relation to the object for experience than that reproduced in the dialectic of enlightenment. In the latter the relation to the object is repeated abstractly but abstraction itself becomes an object in and for experience and is thus returned to its being known in experience. In this dialectic culture can still be the recognition of its formation in and as self-examination. But the culture industry posits itself as lacking any such relation to the object or, thereby, as culture, to itself. It has a relation, rather, to reality as image in what can be mechanically reproduced. As such, within culture as an industry, it is the loss of aura that is reproduced. Or, put differently, in the culture industry image begets image. This marks the end of culture as critique. Indeed, as we will see in a moment, it marks the end of culture as an educational concept. The (non) relation, the immediacy of image and reality, has displaced even its own representation in thinking, namely, that myth is already enlightenment and enlightenment reverts to myth. It has displaced dialectic with a reality freed from political reference. It marks also the fate of philosophy within a notion of culture that is stripped of its formative education. Here representation eschews opposition or negation by rendering all reality equivalent as image. Appearing as liberal democracy, this representation in fact marks an important development in the spirit of Fascism. It liquidates opposition by freeing everything (and everyone) from the illusion, now overcome, of the universal. Image is a form of voyeurism of totality from without, meaning that there is no totality. As such, freed from any dependence upon the object, image is the new political reality, a reality which knows it is liberated from the political *per se*. No wonder then that freedom has greater significance in the choice of TV channels than in voting.

However, the effacing of the dialectic in image and reality does represent its universality to itself, and is therefore also a culture. We will explore this representation now as fossil fuel culture. This means exploring both the representation of culture as freedom and the culture of representation as freedom. It is this complex complicity that both denies culture and commends it.

Fossil fuel culture marks a form of the aestheticization of the political that extends more deeply into representation than that identified by Benjamin in *Trauerspiel* or in mechanical reproduction. The spirit of seventeenth-century Baroque *Trauerspiel* was despair and destruction in the face of desertion, a relation of inner anxiety and outer ruin. The Baroque spirit of the twenty-first century masks destruction behind a freedom *from* desertion. This is the phenomenology of spirit in modern social relations. Unfreedom is experienced as a spirit of mourning which is aberrated in the sense that it is effaced, or, put slightly differently, when the inner and outer correspond to each other in a freedom *from* desertion by the universal. In this phenomenology the inner and the outer are the ideology of ideology and are image and reality, related in such a way as to eschew relation. Freed from a relation to each other, freed from the object *per se*, this aesthetic representation is no longer anxiety, ruin, or intrigue felt as the desertion by God, but rather a representation of absolution from that desertion. This representation is the aesthetic of image as reality. It is culture become the immediacy of the representation of this freedom and it is representation become the immediacy of the culture of this freedom. Together they are the form and content of image and reality. Together they are ideology not of freedom but as freedom.

The 'reality' of this freedom is what I am calling fossil fuel culture. It is not just a way of representing freedom; it is also a way of reproducing itself in and for modern experience, as culture without culture. Its representation is its reproduction; its reproduction is its representation. Fossil fuel culture is the circle that knows no negation, only pure return (and pure returns). This self-sufficiency combines the aesthetic with a categorical imperative, forming a (non) culture that is total. Its real power lies in being the condition of the possibility of everything and in securing fossil fuel freedom from dependence upon or even relation to an object. This freedom is freedom from implication and is made possible by the personal independence that is created by the internal combustion engine in particular, and by the burning of fossil fuels in general. Fossil fuel culture is the fetishism of personal freedom made image and this image become political reality. Without an object which is other than itself fossil fuel culture releases each of us from any relation, debt, guilt, anxiety or fear and trembling. It is the freedom of a godless spirituality, a version of Hegel's spiritual animal kingdom – but not an individuality free from substance by withdrawing from the world, rather, an individuality whose freedom in the world is freedom from substance.

As such, this freedom, or this experience of unfreedom, is actual as the (non) culture of the driver who fills her car up or the consumer who turns on the air conditioning or the central heating. These are the freedoms of fossil fuel culture; freedom to travel without the recognition of nature as other; freedom to shop without the recognition of labour and poverty; freedom as the master who needs no slaves and who knows no slaves; freedom to burn fossil fuels without having to recognize either inner anxiety or outer chaos. Free, because released from implication. Free as voyeur of a negation which is not mine. Hence, traffic jams are caused by everyone except me; I can watch the destruction of the earth's resources knowing that my life is not to blame; I can watch the struggles for freedom knowing they will never be my struggle. This is the modern phenomenology of modernity, where universality vanishes into image, and freedom is freedom from otherness *per se*. It is the logic of civil society *par excellence*. It is not the fetishism of the particular. It is the particular become image and reality, released from the object. The phenomenology of modernity we can say here is absolute freedom from the concept. As such, fossil fuel culture represents and reproduces itself in my freedom as a voyeur of destruction (which is, of course, also my own destruction). Never is the aesthetic of destruction sufficiently related to an object for it to become a critique of this fascism of representation. Never, as I switch on the light or turn on my car engine is the truth of this freedom – the aesthetic of destruction – rendered visible or accountable in relation to itself of therefore to the universal.

Thus my identity as a person, my mastery, consists in my having fossil fuel culture relieve me from all social and political relations. It relieves me from my determination as self *and* other, because it aestheticizes the life and death struggle. Death is reduced to an image, something unreal, something represented in such a way as to have no actual relation to life. Death, and the slave, and the other – the carriers of the meaning of our political education – in fossil fuel culture are entertainment. It means that I am never other because the other is not real. As such I am relieved of any experience in which I learn of myself as the master of fossil fuel culture, or as the destroyer.

This freedom from death will – *is* – destroying itself. The wars, current and future, for control of oil are destined to be the aesthetic of destruction that Benjamin identified. Indeed, riots and wars for oil in the name of freedom point towards an almost certain future. The totality of fossil fuel culture, unmediated by the totality of the negative, as suggested above, is its own categorical imperative. It is an imperative which reproduces itself in an aesthetic of destruction. In fossil fuel culture, destruction *is* freedom.

The immediacy of this imperative, feeding itself on the need which it creates, resembles Adorno's critique of culture as pre-digested 'baby-food'
(1991: 58). Both offer a dialectic of nihilism emancipated from all needs
save those which it reproduces for itself. But fossil fuel culture adds an
important dimension to this totality of ideology. It enjoys the fetishism of
the object as the fetishism of fetishism itself. Freedom is freedom not only
from the object, but also from alienation from the object. As such, fossil
fuel culture echoes Adorno's observation that objects pass 'impotently by'
(1991: 62). 'Nothing happens any more' (1991: 62–63).[6] The decay of aura
has already removed experience from its objects. Image and reality parade
as the aestheticization of the political, and freedom from culture is the new
culture, fossil fuel culture.

We have seen, at the beginning of this century, that fossil fuel culture
claims and will continue to claim the state of emergency and 'restoration'
as its own unquestionable imperative. This freedom, this imperative, is
absolute godless spirituality, and is evil. It has overcome nature yet it is also
in a constant state of emergency in anticipating, knowing, that nature will
only yield finite amounts of freedom. Running out of oil, whether as a
disruption in supplies or as the end of oil reserves, will play itself out as the
allegory of the fallen creature. Fascism will carry the crisis. It will offer the
'sanctuary' (Adorno, 1991: 87) of a dialectic of nihilism, inwardly experienced as the yearning for a restoration of itself with the freedom that is
deserting it, and outwardly carrying out its imperative for restoration in
ruthless fashion such that the dialectic of nihilism becomes the *praxis* of
intrigue. At stake is how fossil fuel culture learns to represent itself as other
to itself. Those who refuse this negation, this real loss of abstract freedom,
will find in a state of emergency the authority to destroy others by protecting themselves. Those who can learn of culture as the representation of
representation will learn of their collaboration in the illusions of fossil fuel
freedoms and will recognize a relation to the universal. But do not be sur-
prised then, when, 'at home', freedom demands armed guards at petrol
stations, and 'abroad', it offers destruction to feed the aesthetic. In what
may prove to be the *coup de grâce* of fascist culture, through the reproduction of destruction on television and the Web, the categorical imperative
of bourgeois freedom will itself be aestheticized. As such, even absolute
destruction will not be recognized as a universal event. Ruin in fossil
fuel culture is the absence of a notion of culture as representation at all. We
are continually learning to enjoy (watching) the recognition that there
is nothing we can do. That, above all else, is the triumph of culture as the

representation of Fascism and the fascism of representation, and as the fate of philosophy.

End of culture

There is a second way in which the spirit of Fascism represents itself; this is as the culture – or, really the lack of culture – of specific forms of philosophy. The term 'post-modern' refers to the state of emergency brought about in and through the dialectic of enlightenment. The totality of the latter is the experience of desertion by the universal and objectivity, and marks philosophy as the site of the ruin. In turn, this absence even of the possibility of resistance produces in consciousness a capitulation to the culture that represents this resignation. The ideology of the ideology of this culture is that it is representation without a notion of itself as culture.[7] Thought is denied its own expression as thinking, the dialectic of enlightenment ceases to '*examine itself*' (Adorno and Horkheimer, 1979: xv) and thought is reduced to predatory voyeurism. Thus the culture of philosophy is the representation of Fascism and the fascism of representation. Or, the same, the culture of philosophy is become representation without dialectic, without negation and without its difficult or aporetic relation to the universal.

As Adorno and Rose both note, representation is essential to philosophy for it is the dialectical relation between thought and being representing itself as thinking, as knowledge, and as philosophy.[8] The 'transcendence of truth beyond the meanings of individual words' (Adorno, 1973: 11), says Adorno, is the work of representation within philosophy. The 'more' is itself a mediation of that which expresses it. It is the relation, the difference, the dialectical experience of the more and 'the in-itself of this more' (1973: 12). But both Rose and Adorno draw attention to the ways in which philosophy 'would abolish representation' (Rose 1996: 55). Rose states, 'the translation of modern metaphysics into ontology involves, first and last, the overcoming of representation as the *imperium* of the modern philosophical subject, and as the false promise of universal politics' (1996: 55). This, she says, converges with '*the inner tendency* of Fascism itself' (1996: 41). Ontology cannot discern between evil and positivity because ontology 'can only read experience as identitarian' (1996: 56). Thus, ontology reads 'the insistence on ground . . . [as] the process involved in the Nazi myth of racial superiority' (1996: 56) and refuses the experience of the modern subject its *lack* of identity, its dialectic of enlightenment. Resignation before the desertion of truth and its consequent evil of posited identity characterizes 'the new ontology' (1996: 56). It cannot distinguish between self-identity as fixed and as fluid because it denies the experience of the relation. Without the experience, evil 'makes itself at home with itself' (Adorno, 1973: 26).

Adorno makes a similar case to Rose. In philosophies of the 'authentic', 'the authority of the absolute is overthrown by absolutized authority' (1973: 5). This form of absolute godless spirituality, complicit with the language that it strips of representational significance, offers itself as a refuge from the false promise of universal politics. However, it is, says Adorno, a refuge where 'a smoldering evil expresses itself as though it were salvation' (1973: 5). Rose notes that the new ontology gives 'Being to beings, who live and die' (Rose, 1996: 55). Adorno, more directly, observes that in relation to a philosophy where 'simply to be there becomes the merit of a thing' (1973: 21), beings could 'hardly do anything other than exist' (1973: 13). The jargon of authenticity marks the state of emergency for philosophy now, not because of the desertion of the universal from the creaturely, but from its absolution from desertion in Being. The year 1933 marks the state of emergency that responds to the ruin of universal politics and the philosophical subject by denying their formative significance. Good and evil, positive and negative, are therein released from their bondage to the autonomous moral subject and retrieved in their authenticity for states of Being. Thus, says Adorno,

> positive and negative are reified prior to living experience, as though they were valid prior to all living experience of them; as though it was not thought that first of all determined what is positive or negative; and as though the course of such determination were not itself the course of negation. (1973: 21)

In terms of education in Hegel, this is to say that the jargon of the authenticity of Being posits the meaning of life and death as a voyeur of their struggle and not as the result of that struggle and the illusions it carries.

Dominant within philosophy then is the effacing of its formation within the baroque spirit of desertion, an effacing which is mourning in denial of itself. The dialectic of enlightenment has been traduced into the ideology of the ideology of philosophy and has resigned itself to the notion of totality that it gives to itself when it is no longer attached to itself as its own object. This fetishism of philosophy is again the inner tendency of Fascism. It destroys opposition, defines totality as equivalence, liquidates experience and the individual, posits illusory being as essence, separates thought from experience, aestheticizes the political, and, through the equivalence of unmediated singularity, reinforces the particularity of bourgeois freedom. In short, it suppresses 'the risk of the universal interest' (Rose, 1996: 62).[9]

So, if the spirit of Fascism dominates not only the political reality of freedom but also its image in and as philosophy, then might we conclude that culture itself, the representation of the relation of state and religion, is fascist through and through? Has modern bourgeois subjectivity become its own ideology, its own duplication? Has the dialectic irretrievably lost its substance, its political significance, to the un-dialectic of the immediacy of image and reality? Are we without an object of experience altogether? If autonomous thinking is resigned, if the dialectic is eschewed in favour of authenticity, and if fossil fuel culture becomes its own ideology of ideology, then the familiar question raises itself – can anything be done? This is the kind of question Adorno felt the need to defend himself against. In 'Resignation', he notes that critical theory was criticized for not producing a programme of action. His response was that resignation lies not in the recognition that individuals are formed and deformed by culture and cannot change this 'merely through an act of their own will' (Adorno, 1991: 171). Rather, resignation is reserved for those who find relief from the cognition of impotence by action. As such, 'the feeling of a new security is purchased with the sacrifice of autonomous thinking' (1991: 174). The question of theory and practice, however, is borne of the same ideology of ideology, the same fascism of representation and representation of Fascism that it would overcome. This is both its strength and its weakness. The fact that we are implicated in political and philosophical cultures is our formation, our deformation and our re-formation. This notion of totality is qualitatively different from a fascist notion of totality as conformity and equivalence, for here culture retrieves itself as its own object.

Any return of the object of thought to itself as thinking, or as our philosophical education, is not the overcoming of fascist culture, but it is the philosophical re-education regarding a notion of totality that fascist culture attributes to itself. To know fascist totality is to know complicity, even in going to the pictures. And to know complicity is to know how to think the dangers, the violence, of guarding our 'particular interests' (Rose, 1996: 62). In the cinema as in the traffic queue, the aestheticization of the political is politicized by the negation of the particular for whom traffic or the audience is everyone except himself. These are strange places to experience the universal, but then, they are cultural experiences. 'We are always staking ourselves in the representation of Fascism and the fascism of representation throughout the range of quotidian practices and cultural rituals' (Rose, 1996: 61). It is an educational matter, then, to learn to comprehend them

differently, not in the kind of cultural studies which only deals in 'close ups
of the things around us by focusing on hidden details of familiar objects'
(Benjamin, 1992: 229) but by the form and content of philosophical thinking that can retain the relation of such experiences to the object as to itself.
Such philosophy is representation and as such is both the fascism of representation and the representation of Fascism.

Illusion

Another way of stating the education described in the previous paragraph
is as education in Hegel. If this education was seen above as able to survive
the end of culture in the quotidian experiences of the traffic queue and the
cinema, and even in turning on a light bulb, it also persists in an equally
unlikely way in Hegelian philosophy. Education in Hegel is present for itself
in the shapes that insist on its disappearance.

   The education in Hegel that forms the substance of each chapter in this
book has its ground in one of Hegel's most difficult ideas, that of the
groundlessness of illusory being. As we will now see, illusory being is death
in life, dependence in independence, and the other in the self. In each of
these relations the illusion is that there is no relation. Education in Hegel
retrieves this relation while recognizing that even such retrieval is grounded
in the groundlessness of illusion. The significance of illusion here is that it
can retrieve for philosophical thought an object where it appears that no
such object exists. In the concrete case of fossil fuel culture – where the
object has been assimilated into the aesthetic of fossil fuel freedom, and
where the paradox of complicity has nothing to set itself against, and where
paradox and complicity thus melt away without substance – this means that
philosophy *can* find an otherness to the totality of its freedom.

   The political significance of illusory being is that the illusory mastery of
the bourgeois is still a substantive self-re-formation, because illusion here is
itself determinative, or educational. The logic of essence in Hegel's *Science
of Logic* is really the logic of the illusions of essence. Being is saved for itself
when essence makes it its own. As such, essence holds itself to be the independence of being. But essence, like all mastery, avoids the dependence of
its mastery upon an other. It avoids its own vulnerability by exporting otherness beyond itself, failing here to recollect otherness within itself. This
illusion is concrete as the subjective reflective thinker, for whom reflection is
autonomy. As such, the mastery of this essence is a positing of life as without
death, or of essence as without nothingness. It is, as we saw in Chapter One
above, life understood from the point of view of the victor in the life and

death struggle. It is really only a non-essence, a merely illusory essence, an illusory mastery. As the truth of the master is the slave so, here, the truth of illusory being is really the nothingness of being that it rejects as other than itself and to itself. In one manifestation the awareness of the illusory foundation of essence here is scepticism. This is because reflection, aware of itself as illusion, believes itself unable to think the truth of anything, for each thought that it holds to be true will be undermined by the groundlessness of all thought. Thus it appears that scepticism is as far as thought can go. The mastery of such scepticism is really a violence against itself, where thought attacks thought. When this is believed to have no educational import for thought, scepticism becomes the aesthetic of destruction. This, as we saw above, characterizes the illusion of fossil fuel freedoms, that totality is null and that actions therefore have no other.

But scepticism is at best only one third of a triadic philosophical education. The harder education, now, is that regarding how illusion can be substantive, and can be educative as self-determinative. This determinate substance is already content[10] within scepticism but not yet recognized or disturbed as such. This content(ment) is carried in the illusion of life as something without nothing, of life without death, of ground without also groundlessness. Reflective subjective essence enjoys this as the idea of itself as completely separate from nothingness. Here, mastery and scepticism are the one reflective freedom. Politically, in fossil fuel culture, this freedom is total in the exclusion of otherness from all sovereign masters. It defines what a 'free' man is, masking the groundlessness of this definition in and by the illusion that fear, death, or other have no part to play here. As such, essence as illusion has no object that can compromise it, for it is related to all externality as freedom from it, and internally, it is related to itself by the absence of such objects. What fossil fuel culture adds to this illusion, as we have seen already, is that externality is in fact no object and that fossil fuel freedom has no responsibilities except to itself. Its actions have no object but themselves, and these are aesthetic.

How, then, can the inherent instability of such political illusion become an object to itself in such a way as to know its freedom re-formed against itself? The philosophical education here is of illusory being learning that, as reflection, it is the reflection of nothing. This contains a crucial ambiguity. As the reflection of *nothing* it is nothing. As the *reflection* of nothing it is something. It is what it is: the reflection of nothing, grounded in groundlessness. This education is open to two misrecognitions of current interest. The first is that this self-mediation, in undermining essence, lends itself to the hope for some form of intersubjective middle between reflective subjects, often conceived as mutual recognition. The second is that this self-mediation is seen to impose itself as an infinitely reproduced difference from itself that eschews all identity thinking, including that grounded in intersubjectivity and the *logos*. Both of these responses are less than and more than the philosophical education that illusion contains. They both posit something other to illusion, rather than see their own complicity within the totality of the other also as illusion. Both responses, the positive overcoming of illusion and the unknowable (excessive) condition of its possibility, essentially posit that of which they are already the return. Suppressing *this* education leaves only what Hegel calls external reflection.

It is to education in Hegel that we now turn in order to understand better the philosophical education that illusion commends. It contains within it immediacy, mediation, and the *Aufhebung*. As immediacy it is the posited sovereignty of the reflective subject. As mediated it is brought into relation with death, with that which is other to itself, and in this case it is where something is brought into relation with nothing. How it understands itself in this relation is the actuality of social and political relations. In fossil fuel culture the relation to death is the relation of freedom without a real object, and where the universal aspect of any action is represented to the voyeur as being without relation to it and thus liberated from responsibility for it. As such, fossil fuel culture is denuded of any educational significance regarding the relation of the universal to personal freedom and hides also the way in which culture achieves this. The truth of fossil fuel culture is that nothing happens. It will require education in Hegel to retrieve what happens when nothing happens.

What happens when nothing happens is that education happens, and this education is both the theory and the practice of the relation of life with death, of self with other, and of freedom with its object. Illusion is just such an education. Essence has an independence that is merely posited: it is illusory being. When illusion learns of itself as illusory being this is not an overcoming of illusion. It is the truth of illusion known as illusion in illusion. This is the nature of the *Aufhebung* here. It knows to know the ground of illusion and the negation of the ground of illusion to be the same groundlessness. This does not resolve the two groundless elements of illusion and its negation. Rather, it is their being learned. What is the 'same' here is that neither of them, neither illusion nor its negation, are the same as themselves. It is in illusion that essence is both already other to itself and that what is other to it is not essence. Illusion is this truth for itself and it is in our philosophical education that illusion is both the theory and practice of this truth – its formation, its negation, and its re-formation in this recollection.

The truth of illusion is the truth of the negation of the negation, the truth that is groundless. It is this notion of truth that can retrieve the missing universal from within the end of culture and within fossil fuel freedom.

Education in Hegel teaches that it is in the illusions of the master in fossil fuel culture that the latent fascism of this objectless political form becomes unstable and collapses. But without the philosophical education that illusion *does* have substance, that in the recollection of illusion something does happen, there will remain only the end of culture, an empty repetition of illusion without meaning. And this latter captures completely the standpoint of fossil fuel culture. Education in Hegel is a re-formed relation to the paradox of contingency and to the other that is hidden within fossil fuel mastery. It asks of us that we learn to do justice to aporia and not to abandon it as a dead end. Doing justice to fossil fuel culture means complicity as education and not, as in the academic workshop, complicity without education. It is the retrieval of such a concept of implication which provides for rather than effaces the relation to the universal.

Nevertheless, the ideology of fossil fuel culture provides the current and most likely the future form and content of representation, of thinking. As the oil runs out, so representation of the universal in fossil fuel freedoms will become increasingly difficult. Each time I drive my car the universal is ideologically represented. Each time I cannot drive my car the universal will assert itself. But without learning how this assertion is *another* representation of freedom, *another* politics, and *another* understanding of thinking, the universal will remain unthinkable within fossil fuel freedom. It is not just a question of new and renewable sources of energy. It is also a question of renewing political and philosophical education regarding the nature of fossil fuel freedom. To renew energy sources in order only to repeat fossil fuel freedom will repeat eternally the crisis that feeds our fascistic desires. There may not be long to wait before the fascism of the representation of fossil fuel culture meets the universal that it eschews in a war for its own survival. Even that, however, may not be enough to retrieve its universal significance from the spectacle of war.

Notes

[1] Though I note that at the time of writing some are arguing that OPEC has exaggerated the levels of oil reserves.

[2] See Tubbs (2005a).

[3] I have explored this double relation in much greater detail as philosophy's higher education. See Tubbs, 2004. It is also the philosophical insight underpinning my study of the philosophy of the teacher in Tubbs (2005b).

[4] The chapter that this is taken from in Rose's *Judaism and Modernity* is also reprinted in Marcus and Nead, (1998) 85–117.

[5] From Adorno, 1991: 159.

[6] This remark is relevant here as a critique of fossil fuel culture but not as a description of education in Hegel.

[7] This is a charge that Rose (1981) makes of Marxism in the final chapter of *Hegel Contra Sociology*.

[8] A case can also be made that for Benjamin representation is the form and the content of the transcendental and the speculative relation of philosophical experience. See, for example, Caygill, 1998, chapter 1.

[9] Author's italics removed.

[10] The double meaning here is intentional.

Chapter 4

Education in Hegel in Derrida

[I]n her [Gillian Rose's] critical engagement with Derrida in particular, there are chapters yet to be written.

(*Wood, 2002: 117*)

Introduction

In this chapter I read education in Hegel alongside and apart from philosophical education in Derrida. This involves looking both at how Derrida extricates philosophy and transformation from absolute spirit, that is, from absolute knowing, and at the kind of education, influenced by his view of absolute spirit, that underpins the idea of *différance*. I will make the case here that *différance* is grounded in a misunderstanding of the nature and character of Hegelian absolute spirit.[1] That is to say, Derrida does not comprehend the absolute in education in Hegel, but he does recognize the importance of philosophy and of aporia within it as transformative. In short, I will argue that Derrida posits the absolute in absolute spirit not as education in Hegel but as a dogma of totality, and because of this he seeks to protect for philosophy what is educational in spirit from its being engulfed in this dogma. The goal of *différance*, therefore, is to retrieve for philosophy the movement of doubling in spirit while rejecting its triadic totality in Hegelian *Aufhebung*. Like many Hegelians before him, Derrida wants the power of aporetic critique without the baggage of the absolute. He wants to keep the content of the form of aporetic education something yet-to-come, something undecideable. In doing so, Derrida takes non-absolute Hegelianism as far as and perhaps further than anyone else in the recent history of Western philosophy.

The chapter is in eight sections. The first speaks of Hegelian hesitations regarding Derridean aporia by way of Richard Beardsworth. This raises considerably what is at stake politically as well as philosophically between Hegel and Derrida in terms of transformation. The second section introduces the idea of transformation in Derrida's philosophy. The third, fourth and fifth sections look to *Glas*, *Of Spirit* and *Rogues*, respectively for clues as to the nature of education that underpins these works. The sixth section explores ways in which the Derridean notion of transformation avoids its totality as complicity and avoids therein the truth of its own spirit. The penultimate section explores fear and sovereignty in Hegelian and Derridean aporetic philosophical education, while a short conclusion returns to Beardsworth's concern about lack of ambition in Hegel. In sum, while it can be seen that Derrida seeks to employ the power of aporetic philosophical education as critique, in fact he avoids its most difficult moment by exporting its open-ness to otherness – it's own otherness and that of others to it – as something beyond the actuality of political education. Derrida always had the opportu-nity to find in *différance* the truth of identity and difference, but, even in returning to reason in later work, he still refused the *Aufhebung* its truth in and as transformation.[2]

Derrida and the political

In his book *Derrida and the Political* (1996) Richard Beardsworth makes the timely warning against seeing Hegel as 'the major philosophical forerunner of twentieth century political terror' (1996: 159) and against the 'common-place of contemporary French philosophy that Hegel is "the" thinker of identity' (1996: 47). Indeed, he defines two ways in which Hegel and Derrida are close by each other. First, *différance* and the *Aufhebung* are both philoso-phies of complicity, working from within the conceptual logic to comprehend in Hegel their fate and in Derrida their being contaminated. 'Both philoso-phies,' he says, 'can be considered as descriptions of the "economies" between law, its violence, the exclusions which violence engenders and the return of what is excluded' (1996: 72). As such, Hegel and Derrida should 'be thought together, their differences articulated, and not placed in oppo-sition' (1996: 72).

The second way in which Beardsworth sees Hegel and Derrida close by each other comes in what he calls his 'hesitation' (1996: 95) regarding Derrida's conceptualizing of the disavowal of time that conditions meta-physics and logic. He asks whether, by returning logic to the aporia of time, Derrida in fact misses the chance for 'transforming' (1996: 96) the logic that suppresses the aporia. Does Derrida risk 'leaving the historic-material determinations of time too "undetermined"' (1996: 96) and in turn leave the promise, the unknowable, appearing 'too formal?' (1996: 154). If so, it is a formality that freezes Derrida's deconstructions of the tradition 'into a finite, but open set of "quasi-transcendental" logics which turn the relation between the human and the technical into a "logic" of supplementarity without history' (1996: 154). This hesitation, Beardsworth notes, is of 'Hegelian inspiration' (1996: 96) and concerns the need for 'Hegelian mediation' (1996: 97).

However, I want also to note that in more recent work Beardsworth's Hegelian hesitations have developed into the need to think the centre between what we might be (religion) and what we are (politics). Philosophy in Hegel, says Beardsworth, is the labour required to know this difference. But how, he asks, is this to be known within a globalized diremption of particular and universal enacted on the one hand as the abstract freedom of the individual in unmediated civil society and, on the other, as the prosaic finite gods of materialism and militarism? He argues that thinking the centre of this global diremption 'may well be beyond human intervention and creativity, but it remains a theoretical and political necessity' (2007: 2).[3] It will require identity and difference to be thought together and not, therefore, as the excess of French thought nor the tragic mourning of recognition as misrecognition that is the causality of fate of Hegelian philosophy. For Beardsworth, if I may put it this way, Hegel's 'grey on grey' is always too late, and Derrida's *différance* is never in time.

I cannot here address directly Beardsworth's case for the centre being constituted as secular political love nor on his strategic use of the early Hegel in doing so. However, I do want to note what he says now regarding his *Derrida and the Political*. In the latter he says, I

> brought Hegel and Derrida together, at least initially, through the thinking of aporia. I am no longer in agreement with this position. I consider the focus upon aporia intellectually sophisticated but unhelpful and unambitious with regard to the matter at hand: world politics (including religion), global capitalism, and the reinvention of democracy. (2007: 14)

I have included these comments for the following reason. In *Derrida and the Political* Beardsworth reads Hegel and Derrida together and apart through the question of mediation. Now, ten years later, he recalls them together through aporia, but finds similar weaknesses in both regarding the ambition for transformation. This sets me a doubly difficult problem, namely, to show how aporia is central to Hegel and Derrida, but also to distinguish the significance and the ambition they attach to philosophy as the thinking of this aporia. The second problem is the harder one, for the

charge that aporetic education is unambitious goes to the heart of education in Hegel. It asks, bluntly, is recollection, the grey in grey, too unambitious
and, in a sense, a reduction of critique to tragic nostalgia? Each of the chapters in this book addresses this in some way, and in each of them I have been
conscious of the charge of education in Hegel as politically unambitious.
I will also address this charge directly towards the end of this chapter.

Derridean education

The Derridean philosophical project – and despite the fact that such a
description might appear to invoke a form of closure, there is a Derridean
project – holds within itself the claim that 'iteration alters: something new
takes place' (Derrida, 1988: 40). The iterability of an element 'divides its
own identity a priori' (1988: 53), and ensures 'a minimal remainder . . . in
order that the identity of the *selfsame* be repeatable and identifiable *in,
through*, and even *in view of* its alteration' (1988: 53).[4] Hence, the structure
of iteration 'implies *both* identity *and* difference' (1988: 53).[5] The re-marked
is what is remarkable. Since it carries the remarkable with it, and since the
remainder is not 'a full or fulfilling presence' (1988: 53), iterability is the
Derridean critique of identity *per se*. Iteration, *différance* and its remarkable
return without loss, are therefore 'a differential structure escaping the logic
of presence or the (simple or dialectical) opposition of presence and
absence, upon which the idea of permanence depends' (1988: 53). Iterability, therefore, is not negative, for negativity presupposes a repose of identity
as lost. Against this, *différance* is a structural theme carried in and as 'the
positive condition of the emergence of the mark. It is iterability itself . . .
passing between the *re-* of the repeated and the *re-* of the repeating, travers-
ing and transforming repetition' (1988: 53). It is this open-endedness that
draws support from many quarters for Derrida. Events are by definition
already unfulfilled; understanding is already the impermanence of iterability; concepts are already doubled in the structural difference that is their
very possibility. 'I will go even further,' says Derrida: 'the structure of the
remainder, implying alteration, renders all absolute permanence impossible. Ultimately remaining and permanence are incompatible' (1988: 54).

This question of education is lived by Derrida in the feeling of 'loss without return' (Derrida, 1995: 144). 'I am fortunate,' he says, for

I do not have any negative experience in this sense; everything that I live
. . . is such that I would be capable of wishing it to start over again eternally. This is an affirmative desire in the sense in which Nietzsche defined

the eternal return in its relation to desire: let everything return eternally. (1995: 144)

In eschewing this return as negative, here, Derrida hopes to set free this form of movement and transformation from any arrogance that it can also be its own content. There is a stoicism here in that decisions that surrender to divisibility and undecideability are 'the only decisions possible: impossible ones' (1995: 147). There is also a scepticism, for in writing, as in saying, and in theory as in practice,

> the most firmly decided is the decision to maintain the greatest possible tension between the two poles of the contradiction . . . what is the most decided is the will not to give up one or the other . . . it is a matter of affirming the most tense, most intense difference possible between the two extremes (1995: 151)

or of *suspending* the closure of one by the other. This also, at times, characterizes Derrida's relation to Hegel. For example, Derrida acknowledges his sharing the effect called philosophy with Hegel. Hegel, he says, may well be the 'express form' (1995: 140) of the desire for and project of absolute knowledge, but 'I seek it just like everyone else' (1995: 141). And in 'Violence and Metaphysics' Derrida says that, in thinking the equivocal in speculation that is 'original and irreducible' (Derrida, 1978: 113), and in the need to 'accommodate duplicity and difference within speculation' (1978: 113), no one 'has attempted this more profoundly than Hegel' (1978: 113).

I want now in the following three sections to explore ways in which education plays a part in Derrida's work. I will look at *Glas*, *Of Spirit* and *Rogues*, respectively to see how each invokes a form or forms of transformation.

Glas

Glas provokes the autoimmunity of Hegelian *Aufhebung* beyond itself in excess of the totality of difference-opposition in modern Western philosophy. In doing so Derrida presents us with a remarkable spiritual exercise in complicity in order to illustrate how close by each other the transformation of *différance* and the education of *Geist* really are. As we will see, his strategy here is to prioritize the totality of spirit in order to find *différance* within it. There is still the claim of *différance* as the to-come, but the strategy here for transformation is to read *différance* as much within the totality of *Geist* as possible.

At the beginning of *Glas* Derrida grants totality to Hegel, and admits that to begin *Glas* is already, always not to have 'yet read, heard or understood Hegel' (Derrida, 1986: 4), but also, at the same time, to be already, always, within Hegel in that lack of reading, hearing or understanding. 'So, already, one would be found entrained in the circle of the Hegelian beginning' (1986: 4). Yet, says Derrida, if the *Aufhebung* is 'the schema of the internal division, of self-differentiation as self-determination and self-production of the concept' (1986: 7) how, then, can it also leave this family relation for the ethical life of work and law? Is there room here for the ambiguity of a bastard offspring, both within and without the family, 'that will have to feign to follow naturally the circle of the family?' (1986: 6). If so, how will this bastard know itself? Within the family there is a pressure of belonging that is therefore accompanied by a pressure to belong. Family pressure (*Trieb*) is already a division of inner and outer, even in being the family. Philosophy is the (unwelcome) calculation of this division, a calculation grounded – presupposed – in the appearance of division or pressure as *opposition*. The latter is felt as 'a lack [that] I try to fill up' (1986: 25). 'To relieve the terms of the opposition, the effects of the division' (1986: 95) is the unique inter-est of philosophy. *Glas* traces the relation of this relief to its condition of possibility in difference-opposition.[6]

Derrida's critique here is not only of philosophy as a calculation of relief from opposition. It is also a critique of the way philosophy assumes opposition and its relief as its *logos*. This is the central argument of *Glas*. Spirit may claim itself as this speculative circular relation but in fact philosophy's complicity with opposition, a complicity that sees them claim the whole for themselves, is a suppression of the pressure of the family circle. Indeed, not just a suppression, but a relief of this family pressure in the calculation of opposition and its overcoming. This relief is philosophy's and Hegel's *Aufhebung*. Starting from opposition, it calculates resolution around the need to belong, and issues a relief, a copulation and a copula of its own that in erasing pressure claims beginning, end and working middle as its own. The bastard performs here an 'anti-erection' (1986: 26) or an 'upside-down erection' (1986: 81). He does not simply reproduce (family, pressure); he reproduces in such a way as to reclaim the natural, to ingest it as his own merely undeveloped moment. This is, therefore, a Derridean critique of the Hegelian *Aufhebung*. The extent to which it is also a critique of recollec-tion and education in Hegel we will return to in due course.

The development of this *Aufhebung* as anti-erection sees the family structure overturned in and by this new conceptual logic of relief and ingestion.
Where pressure held the family together, speculative relief rebuilds the
family from within opposition. A family built on the principle of the bastard
takes a recognizably contradictory and speculative form. 'The son is son
only in his ability to become father, his ability to supply or relieve the father,
in his occupying his place by becoming the father of the father, that is, of
the son's son. A father is always his grandfather and his son his own grand-
son' (1986: 81). In the same way, Derrida relieves Hegel's family pressure.
The young Hegel who anticipates Hegelianism and completes Hegelianism
is not only the adolescent become mature, but is where 'the Hegelian tree
is also turned over; the old Hegel is the young Hegel's father only in order
to have been his son, his great-grandson' (1986: 84).

As an example of family pressure relieved in this way Derrida turns to the
role of the sister in Hegelian immediate ethical life, and in particular to the
opposition between the 'law of singularity and the law of universality' (1986:
142). Human law is male, public, and visible; it is the activity of the known
and its being known. Divine law is 'the law of woman' (1986: 142), more
natural, nocturnal, hidden. The natural moment of pure singularity for the
brother who does not yet know the 'universality-producing labour in the
city' (1986: 143) is death. But even here there is work in the form of mourning that, 'as the economy of the dead' (1986, 143), retrieves/returns nature
to spirit. Denied burial, as in *Antigone*, the two laws come into conflict. Yet
Derrida criticizes Hegel's reading here in the *Phenomenology* as being based
exclusively on a Western Greek family model and, consequently, restricting
itself only to a limited number of relations. This plays itself out as two antinomical family relations; one the conjugal relation from which nothing
leaves, and one the parental relation whose outpouring of nature cannot
return. Of greater interest to Derrida is 'the infinite superiority of the bond
between brother and sister' (1986: 148). Here brother and sister are not
related through desire, nor through recognition. They are related neither
as male and female, nor as activity and passivity, nor as civic persons. How
then can they be naturally related to each other without desire or dependency? Hegel's answer is that the sister is the 'highest intuitive awareness of
what is ethical' (Hegel, 1977: 274), both natural and free. Yet this highest
intuitive awareness is relieved within the system, ingested by the *Aufhebung*
that sees the brother become citizen and the sister get married. Or, in other
words, difference is again relieved as opposition, or *différance* is present only as
the male perspective and as the work of knowledge. Derrida states here that

the opposition between difference and qualitative diversity is a hinge of the greater Logic. Diversity is a moment of difference, an indifferent difference, an external difference, without opposition. As long as the two moments of difference (identity and difference since identity differs, as identity) are in relationship only to themselves and not to the other, as long as identity does not oppose itself to difference or difference to identity, there is diversity. So diversity is a moment both of difference and identity, it being understood, very expressly, that difference is the whole *and* its own proper moment. (1986: 168)

But, he continues, when natural difference is overcome then 'we pass on to difference *as opposition*' (1986: 168). Only here is diversity now its own seed, and thus autoimmune in 'opening itself to negativity and in becoming opposition' (1986: 168). This is to deconstruct opposition, then, to find the condition of its possibility in *différance*, and not in desire in general. There is no desire 'in general' (1986: 169) prior to difference and identity as opposition. Derrida here rules out any a priori transcendental or immediate-natural difference that is not already 'difference-opposition' (1986: 168). This is the significance for philosophy of *différance as* philosophy. *Différance* is always already opposition, and all reconciliation is by necessity tragic. Ethical life is already culpability in difference-opposition.

Derrida is clear about the thesis that *Glas* carries.

Whether it be a matter of ferment or fervour, the tumultuous opposition of the two 'principles' is always at work: the feminine (night and natural silence of substance) and the masculine (light, *logos* of self-consciousness, becoming-subject of substance). This opposition, like opposition in general, will have been at once the manifestation of difference. . . *and* the process of its effacement or its reappropriation. As soon as difference determines itself, it determines itself as opposition; it manifests itself to be sure, but its manifestation is at the same time . . . the reduction of difference, of the remain(s), of the gap. That is the thesis. (1986: 235–36)

This is Derrida's reading of the totality of Hegelian *Aufhebung*. Its starting point is an opposition that, as the reheating of the remains, seeks therein also to assimilate them, 'to cook, eat, gulp down, interiorize the remain(s) without remains' (1986: 236). The crumbs that are left are themselves appropriated in the Last Supper where opposition determines itself such that nothing shall go to waste; there shall be no remains: *Sa*. Absolute knowing.

In *Glas*, then, it is the status assigned to difference-opposition that separates Derrida from Hegel. Derrida sees difference-opposition in Hegel as absolute and self-completing in *Geist*. For Derrida, however, *différance* is the manifestation of the event,[7] the 'annulus of exchange' (1986: 242), which, in keeping open the remain(s) of difference as opposition, guards the present against the closure of the to-come. *Différance* therefore is not just the 'circle of circles' (1986: 245), it is also a spiral capable of transforming closure into the openness of the to-come.

The architecture of *Glas* also sees *Geist* prioritized, something that is necessary to represent both the totality of *Geist* and its remain(s). Spirit re-heats the remains and rises from nature as 'the phallic column' (1986: 248) on each page. *Différance* is present in the rising as that which 'does not let itself be thought by the dialectics to which it, however, gives rise' (1986: 243). It is the 'singular repercussion of interiority in exteriority' (1986: 250). It is *Glas*. However, *Geist* is also prioritized in the architecture of *Glas* in a further way. The beginning of *Glas*, as we saw, is already Hegel. The end of *Glas*, now, is also Hegel. To be consistent to the totality of difference-opposition in and as *Glas*, ethical life must triumph again over nature in order to arrive at what the family was – is – at the beginning. Hegelian totality encompasses *Glas* completely for now it is clear that *Glas* has to be Hegelian to be able to begin at all. At the moment when nature is relieved by subjectivity, by 'man, free, *self-knowing spirit*' (1986: 256),[8] it is the time for pressure and relief to discuss their differences. It is time for the Dionysian circle to meet the Christian circle and to converse regarding its (their) relation. But such a discussion 'runs to its ruin for it counted without . . . Hegel' (1986: 262–1),[9] who returns the remain(s) to nature and spirit (again). What remains for us are the remains which we 'will not have been able to think without him. For us, here, now: these words are citations, already, always, we will have learned that from him' (1986: 1), again.

In this way, *Glas* is a remarkable suspension not only of the autoimmunity of *Geist*, but also of the differences between *Geist* and *différance*.[10] The whole circle of *Glas* is Hegelian; the columns that emerge from nature on each page are the triumph of calculation rising from reheating the remain(s). But its resonance, its suppressed other that is other to difference-opposition while also being in it, is *Glas*. In this sense *Glas* is the totality of the to-come that is resonant even within the totality of Hegelian *Aufhebung*, a totality that cannot be avoided if *différance* is to be (un)known. *Glas*, in its totality beyond its totality – even in the to-come of *Geist* – is also *différance*. The suspension of *Geist* and *différance* here is the remarkable, an iteration that alters and wherein something new takes place. It is, we might say, a Derridean form of *Aufhebung*. It marks excess as well as completion as the truth of the totality of *Geist*, and does so unmistakably around the idea of *différance* which carries this movement as alteration, that is, as philosophical education.

Of Spirit

I want now to explore how this totality of *Geist* as an autoimmunity that exceeds itself pertains to political critique in *Of Spirit*. In particular, I want to look at how Derrida sees the complicity of *différance* within *Geist* is first maintained by Heidegger but then abandoned. The strategy of suspension is here referred to by Derrida as 'doubling' and it is in doubling that transformation is carried here.

Of Spirit is divided into three climactic moments: the strategy of doubling of metaphysics and *Dasein* in *Being and Time* and the Rectoral Address; the strategy of undoubling in the *Introduction to Metaphysics* of 1935; and the strategy of gathering together in 1953. A brief word, now, on each of these three moments.

First, Derrida notes that in *Being and Time* Heidegger is clear that he must avoid the term spirit because, in its Cartesian-Hegelian heritage, *Geist* has itself avoided – blocked – 'any interrogation on the Being of *Dasein*' (Derrida, 1987: 18). This Heidegger achieves in 1927, by re-marking it in inverted commas. Derrida comments here that 'spirit' within inverted commas allows its remainder, its repetition to be salvaged. Heidegger avoids the traditional concept of spirit ('spirit') by avoiding avoiding its being doubled. In this doubling of avoiding avoiding 'spirit returns' (1987: 23) in the priority of the question.

In contrast, but for Derrida of the same strategy, the Rectoral Address of 1933 defines spirit without inverted commas, which Derrida reads as a doubling or inversion of the doubling within inverted commas in 1927. If the latter is a more recognizable form of opposition to identity, that is, 'spirit,' the former – inverting the inversion – is altogether more disturbing, more risky and more easily misread for the strategy of inverting inversion appears not to be an opposition at all. Thus, says Derrida, and on the one hand, in advancing spirit without inverted commas in the Address Heidegger 'spiritualizes National Socialism' (1987: 39), conferring 'elevated spiritual legitimacy' (1987: 39) upon it; and, Derrida adds, 'one could reproach him for this' (1987: 39). Indeed. But, and on the other hand, Derrida inverts this, saying that 'by taking the risk of spiritualizing nazism, he might have been trying to absolve or save it by marking it with this affirmation' (1987: 39). In other words, spiritual *Dasein* marked by metaphysical dogmas of nature, biology and race is re-marked, doubled, precisely by the removal of the quotation marks. This haunting of spirit by 'spirit' says Derrida, 'sets apart Heidegger's commitment and breaks an affiliation' (1987: 39). Derrida's strategy here is to read Heidegger's comments within the totality of *Geist* and its difference-opposition. This gives political critique a fundamental ambivalence as suspension, prioritizing always that which is being suppressed or hidden. This, says Derrida, is 'because one cannot demarcate oneself from biologism, from naturalism, from racism in its genetic form, one cannot be *opposed* to them except by reinscribing spirit in an oppositional determination (1987: 39). There is no political position that lies outside this spiritual complicity, outside the doubling of *Geist* that is metaphysics and opposition to metaphysics. One can seek to avoid complicity by choosing 'spirit' or spirit, but to choose is to be compromised no matter what one chooses.[11] In response Derrida reveals an insight into the implications for political opposition of doubling within complicity and complicity within doubling. 'Even if all forms of complicity are not equivalent, they are *irreducible*. The question of knowing which is the least grave of these forms of complicity is always there – its urgency and its seriousness could not be over-stressed – but it will never dissolve the irreducibility of this fact' (1987: 40). Note here that Derrida makes a similar point in *Limited Inc*, saying 'if, as I believe, violence remains in fact (almost) ineradicable [in academic discourse] its analysis and the most refined, ingenious account of its conditions will be the least violent gestures, perhaps even nonviolent, and in any case those which constitute most to transforming the legal-ethical-political rules' (1988: 112). Here Derrida clearly identifies the strategy of doubling as making transformative judgements possible.

The second seminal moment in *Of Spirit* concerns Heidegger's definition of spirit in 1935 in his *Introduction to Metaphysics*. Here, Heidegger neither doubles Hegelian *Geist* with *Dasein*, nor breaks the attachment of spiritual *Dasein* to metaphysics. Instead, Heidegger quotes himself on spirit from the Rectoral Address but in doing so omits the one set of inverted commas that had been put around spirit in the original text. The sentence in question states in the Address that 'spirit' is not mere sagacity or rational tool, rather spirit (without inverted commas) is resolution. When this definition of spirit is quoted by Heidegger from his own speech the inverted commas around the first spirit are removed. This strategy Derrida calls 'spectacular' (1987: 66) and a revision 'passed over in silence' (1987: 66).[12] Even if it is inadvertent, it is, he says, still 'an invisible crossing-out' (1987: 67) of a doubling. If Derrida is right, then both in *Being and Time* and in the Address, and in accord with the priority of the question, Heidegger doubles both spirits. But now, in the *Introduction to Metaphysics*, removing the inverted commas around metaphysical *Geist* erases the differentiation between metaphysics and *Dasein* and erases the priority of the question.

To those who would find in Derrida's extended footnote in *Of Spirit* a retraction of the priority of the question in favour of an originary ethics[13] we should note that, in fact Derrida redoubles any strategy of an *Umkehrung*, of a turning that might 'seem to dictate a new *order*' (1987: 131). Any such turning that tried to remove 'the remnant of *Aufklärung* which still slumbered in the privilege of the question' (1987: 131) would be doubled in the attempt. Here Derrida retains the priority of the Hegelian *Aufhebung* and the totality of spirit in/as opposition. Thus, for Derrida everything cannot be re-commenced; even if thinking, late on as it were, permits the path travelled to be seen, even if one can re-trace one's steps, this 'return does not signify a new departure, from a new principle or some degree zero' (1987: 132).[14] The footnote avoids avoiding any effacement of *Geist* by remaining within the 'law of the most radical questioning' (1987: 131). This consistency of complicity is marked and re-marked for Derrida by the equivocation of *Geist* that is 'always haunted by its *Geist*' (1987: 40). The phantom of metaphysics 'always returns' (1987: 40) and *Geist* is 'the most fatal figure of this *revenance*' (1987: 40). This is for Derrida what Heidegger can never avoid, 'the unavoidable itself – spirit's double, *Geist* as the *Geist* of *Geist*, spirit as spirit of the spirit which always comes with its double. Spirit is its double' (1987: 41) and is a double that 'can never be separated from the single' (1987: 40).

The third seminal moment in *Of Spirit* is Derrida's discussion of Heidegger's move from *Geist* to *geistlich* in his thoughts on Trakl's 'spirit in flames' (1987: 85) and on spirit which inflames. Here, political opposition within the complicity of doubling, re-marked by inverted commas and by inverting inverted commas, is no longer present. Now Heidegger carries Trakl's statements in opposition to his (Heidegger's) former equivocation within the complicity of political opposition. No longer doubled within the priority of the question, now, in 1953, spirit is the originarity of the promise, the pledge, the event. Again, Derrida's concern and priority is the extent to which 'this supplement of originarity . . . precedes or exceeds questioning itself' (1987: 90), or, in the terms we are exploring here, the extent to which it avoids metaphysical *Geist*. In short, Derrida argues that the *Geist* that *geistlich* now replaces is merely 'a crudely typecast form of the metaphysico-Platonic tradition' (1987: 95), and, failing to avoid avoiding Hegelian totality, in fact confirms 'a metaphysics of evil, a metaphysics of the will' (1987: 102).

Doubling in *Of Spirit*, then, acts as suspension does in *Glas*. Doubling is able to hold in tension the totality of metaphysics of *Geist and* the to-come that is resonant in that totality in order to effect the transformation that re-marks of *différance*. The Heidegger of 1927–1933 is the Heidegger of this suspension. The Heidegger of 1935–1953 is the Heidegger of the anti-metaphysical and therefore metaphysical dogma of *geistlich*. Derrida maintains the domination of the totality of difference-opposition which Heidegger, he says, 'brutally sends [. . .] packing' (1987: 95). Where Derrida prioritizes the autoimmunity of *Geist* in order to be consistent with its totality, Heidegger simply avoids it, and therein avoids the transformative significance of such autoimmunity.

Rogues

We now turn to one of Derrida's later works, *Rogues*, for a third illustration of transformation in Derridean philosophy. In *Rogues* the concept of auto-immunity is central to Derrida's examination of democracy. At the heart of democracy there is an ambivalence that must be honoured. On the one hand, democracy must protect itself from those who would harm it. This threat can come from within the democracy or from without. Either way, this protection has a feature that moves democracy from being an immune system to an autoimmunity. Since it is part of the freedom of democracy to allow itself to be harmed by itself, it is by its very nature opposed to itself as an autoimmune disorder. When democracy protects itself it attacks itself.

This is a simple enough aporia of self-opposition. But in describing democracy in this way Derrida also has in mind a more important observation. The reality of the autoimmune democracy is that in protecting itself, the 'itself' that it protects is not democracy. Autoimmunity means that democracy is always yet-to-come. Because the protection of democracy is also against itself, it is never a present democracy. It is, rather, 'the interminable adjournment of the present of democracy' (Derrida, 2005: 38). Thus, according to its own ambivalent nature democracy defers itself, differs from itself. This, as we have seen above, is its *différance*. One can say here that whatever educational significance was carried by *différance* and deconstruction in earlier work, it is now also part of the Derridean notion of autoimmunity.

We noted above Derrida's comment that philosophical critique 'is a matter of affirming the most tense, the most intense difference possible between the two extremes' (Derrida, 1995: 151) of a totality and its deferral. We also saw above how Derrida argues that this thinking of *différance* in iterability transforms both totalities in leaving them open to judgements regarding 'the least grave' (Derrida, 1987: 40) of the ways in which deferral is avoided. The example Derrida gives in *Rogues* is the democracy of the United Nations and the way in which the Security Council works as autoimmunity. The Security Council permanently abuses democracy in order to protect democracy. Little philosophical sophistication is needed for those who experience autoimmunity as their being demonized, and, indeed, by the 'devil' himself. This was the view of Hugo Chavez (26 September 2006) when he said at the UN that President Bush 'came here as if he were the owner of the world' but that he was in fact the devil and had left a stench of sulphur after his address the previous day, and of Mahmoud Ahmadinejad who said in the same session, 'as long as the UN Security Council is unable to act on behalf of the entire international community in a transparent, just and democratic manner, it will never be legitimate or effective.'

But as we have already seen above, Derrida's critique of a totality is never as simple as merely pointing out inequalities of power, although this is an important element of deconstruction. In *Rogues* as elsewhere there is a totality of complicity that is more than mere opposition. It is already the case, for example, that the names of Chavez and Ahmadinejad represent the threat to democracy that democracy needs to protect itself against. This is an interminable circle in which the opposition of each 'demon' to the other has its justification. As foes they are the erasure of *différance* because both have their legitimacy in the totality of difference-opposition. This totality of autoimmunity is a powerful example of when and how *différance* is political critique, critique, that is, of this totality and this erasure. In *différance* the Security Council and its opponents can be thought together as the suspension of its (i.e. of *différance's*) erasure. *Différance* here is the deferral of its own deferral, or, in this example, the deferral of the deferral of democracy. This shares its aim with the strategy of doubling in *Of Spirit* and with the architecture of *Glas*. In this example it does justice to the injustice of present democracy. *Différance* here, as the excess of its autoimmunity, presents democracy to itself and leaves open the idea of democracy to-come. This is democracy present within its deferral, and is again where deferral is transformative, altering even as it repeats itself.

But there is an added twist in *Rogues* to the strategy of suspension and alteration. Now, towards the end of his life, Derrida gives priority to *reason* in a way significantly different from his earlier work.[15] Derrida argues here for increased vigilance regarding the changes that the autoimmunity of difference-opposition holds for the world as a whole. Gone is the rational and the very visible form of autoimmune calculation of the Cold War that sat at the precipice of mutually assured destruction in order to avoid mass suicide.[16]

This has been replaced now by a new, more violent, less visibly autoimmune terror and violence. This consists in wars against rogue states, wars that break the very international law that they claim to be defending against those who break it. The excess of the autoimmunity of sovereign state power that can defer the hegemonic rationalizations for terror against terror is weak in comparison to the totality it defers. When Derrida says that the rationalizations employed to justify autoimmune suicide, for example, that of national security, must 'not be allowed to take us unawares' (2005: 157), he is saying that we must think the deferral of such rationalizations. But, and here is the new emphasis, to think this deferral of sovereign rationalizations is to think *rationally* against them. It is to the autoimmunity of reason that Derrida now turns for the strategy of doubling and transformation. We must, he says, sometimes 'in the name of reason, be suspicious of rationalizations' (2005: 157). We must, in the name of reason, call into question – defer – all of the logics of suicidal sovereignty. We must erode the ontotheological rationalizations of sovereignty and with it the suicidal right to undermine law in order to protect it.

This is the same struggle with totality as difference-opposition that Derrida has always been waging. He has always sought to use aporia and autoimmunity against themselves but in a way different from their appearance within difference-opposition. What is mere contradiction in the latter is transformative *différance* in the former. Now, however, he is prepared to name the two different kinds of reason that are at play here. He is ready to make explicit the rational difference between excess and difference-opposition that has always been implicit in his theorizing. Since this difference (and sameness) of *différance* has always been the gesture wherein transformation occurs we must say also that Derrida is now prepared to name the transformative character of *différance* as rational. He calls the aporia of difference-opposition mere rationalization, and the aporia of *différance* he calls reasonableness, vulnerable non-sovereignty and (a different conception of) God. Vulnerable non-sovereignty opposes sovereignty from within according to the latter's own suicidal tendency. It is distinguished from what it opposes and how it opposes precisely because it lacks the sovereignty of suicide. It is suicide without sovereignty, and is a vulnerability without autoimmune rationalization. It is 'the name of a God [that] would allow us to think something else, for example a vulnerable non-sovereignty, one that suffers and is divisible, one that is mortal even, capable of contradicting itself or of repenting . . . it would be a completely different story, perhaps even the story of a God who deconstructs himself in his ipseity' (2005: 157). This vulnerable non-sovereignty, says Derrida, is what is happening today. 'It *is* and it *makes* history through the anxiety-provoking turmoil we are currently undergoing' (2005: 157).

But, as always, the relation of the two kinds of reason is no simple sense of opposition. Were it just one unconditional sovereignty opposing another unconditional sovereignty this would not be deferral, but only more differ-ence-opposition. What, then, characterizes deferral now as non-sovereign and vulnerable reason? It is characterized by the responsibility to be reason-able, to prefer the reasonable, in the opposition between two antinomic rationalizations, and in its being 'irreducible to the rational it exceeds' (2005: 158). It strives for justice across aporias in giving an account of the impossible and the incalculable.

Even here, however, Derrida says he feels he is not immune to the auto-immunity of a regulative Kantian sovereign rationalization. The 'last resort' (2005: 83) of a regulative Idea is something 'I cannot swear that I will not one day give in to' (2005: 83). He would succumb, perhaps, if the to-come carried in non-sovereign reason fails to be transformative in and as 'the cre-ation of an international juridico-political space that, without doing away with every reference to sovereignty, never stops innovating and inventing new distributions and forms of sharing, new divisions of sovereignty' (2005: 87). In other words, a Kantian imperative might be needed if *différance* fails to transform the space that it also opens, a concern we saw above in Beardsworth's hesitations.

Avoiding education in Hegel

In summary then we have followed the idea of transformation as education in Derrida from its statement in *Limited Inc* through three different shapes that it takes. In *Glas* we saw Derrida evoke the totality of spirit in order to do justice to the excess of spirit. His strategy here was to give priority to spirit and to difference-opposition in both architecture and content in order that its totality speaks of itself beyond itself. *Of Spirit*, on the other hand, gives priority to excess in order to expose the doubling and the non-doubling of spirit. He invokes excess in order to do justice to the autoimmunity of spirit, to the totality of its complicity, and to the impossibility of this totality in and through its being doubled. Both strategies aim to do justice to *différance* as transformative. Finally, in *Rogues*, *différance* is seen to be the gesture of a non-sovereign reason, a reason/*différance*, in contrast to the rationaliza-tions of sovereignty that are decidedly unreasonable in their suicidal nature. The aim of *Rogues* is still to do justice to the to-come and the undecideable, but this time by prioritizing the transformative qualities of reasonableness over autoimmune irrationality.

I want now to argue that in fact the one thing Derrida is not truly open to is the truth of transformation in aporetic philosophical education. This takes us to the differences, still together and apart, between Hegel and Derrida on the nature of transformation in aporia, differences which are themselves grounded in presuppositions of knowing and/or not-knowing the absolute or absolute spirit.

The character of transformation in Derrida is that it has all the instability of aporetic spirit, seen in *Glas* and in *Of Spirit*, but with none of the baggage of the absolute that attends spirit in Hegel. This gives the appearance that Derridean transformation is radically open-ended in comparison to Hegelian *Aufhebung* especially when the latter is (mis)understood as the resolution or synthesis or relief of competing opposites. The fluidity of education in Derrida is not dependent upon negation or loss, nor upon reconciliation. Instead, the movement of *différance* is an effect of identity, not an opposition of non-identity. The transformative import of *différance* is in its trace of the impossible within the autoimmunity of identity. This is to come to understand the world differently.

In *Rogues*, as we saw, transformation is stated in rational terms, as the transformation that inheres in 'the fragile difference between the *rational* and the *reasonable*' (2005: 159). Here we might expect Hegelian *Aufhebung* and Derridean aporetic education to converge further. Hegel has, after all, always been working with two different types of reason: abstract reason and philosophical reason. Abstract reason resembles the sovereignty of rationalization in Derrida and philosophical reason resembles the reasonableness that massively compromises such rationalization. Further, where Derrida in *Rogues* turns to the character of reason as vulnerable and mortal, and even divine, it is the case as we saw above in Chapter 1, that the master/slave relation in the *Phenomenology of Spirit* is the template in Hegel for the transformative relationship of power and its vulnerability. But any suggestion now that the aporetic philosophies of Hegel and Derrida are commensurable in this respect is absolutely unsustainable. The reason is, that precisely where Derrida in *Rogues* articulates transformation in and as the concept of reason/*différance*, spirit is nowhere to be seen. Just when Derrida finally turns to reason to think through the antinomies of power, and indeed in terms of (a different) God, his previous strategy of using spirit as the totality of this thinking is dropped, an avoidance we might say here, that is passed over in silence.

Why is it that reason/*différance* and spirit cannot be thought together by Derrida in *Rogues?* Why is he willing to work with spirit when *différance* is not explicitly gestured as reasonableness, and equally unwilling to work with spirit when rational non-sovereignty defines *différance* and the to-come? The answer to this is that *différance* (and reason/*différance*) as Derrida conceives it must not know itself as its own content. The emphasis placed on reason in *Rogues* makes it especially vulnerable to having its own content in spirit, and in absolute knowing. But for Derrida, reason/*différance* must not be able to know itself, for in doing so it would make transformation its own truth; knowable; *Sa.* It is this presupposition that underpins the Derridean project. Spirit in Hegel has always been both the form and the content of the autoimmunity of sovereignty. This is what spirit is. Indeed, this is what is educative in both the life and death relation and the master/slave relation as education in Hegel presents them. Life is autoimmune. It opposes itself even as it lives, for everything it does brings death closer. Sovereignty is also autoimmune. In the master/slave relation the absolute sovereignty of the master is exposed as autoimmune by his dependence upon the slave. The slave, in turn, is absolute vulnerability and non-sovereignty. Life and death, and master and slave are components of a spiritual education that has aporia as its educative form and content. Spirit is this form and content, and absolute spirit is this form and content in and as learning, as spirit's formative and substantial education about itself. This educative *truth* of death in life and of non-sovereignty in sovereignty is exactly what Derrida avoids for autoimmunity on behalf of spirit. Derrida is happy for spirit to double itself but not that it should know itself in this doubling. This doubling can be a transformation of spirit in learning about its excess, its to-come, and its radical undecideability, but it cannot be a transformation that is formative of and substantial as spirit's own education regarding itself. In education in Hegel, however, it is because spirit is both the form *and* content of death in life and of sovereignty attacking itself, that it is also transformative in and of itself, transformative of sovereignty from within and not prejudged by a view from without that spirit formed in this way compromises truth in an unacceptably dogmatic way. The Derridean grounding of *différance* against absolute spirit here is in the presupposition of what is and is not acceptable in the thinking of truth.

As we have seen, Derrida has been comfortable to work with the auto-immunity of spirit. The brilliance of *Glas* is that it seeks not to avoid the circle of spirit. Yet, even here, the reading of the *Aufhebung* as relief eschews the truth and totality of spirit as always in struggle without relief. Relief is as unrelieved as everything else in the totality of *Geist. This* is what is learned in and as philosophy in education in Hegel. The event of the to-come is in fact relief for Derrida from what is deemed or presupposed to be unacceptable in absolute spirit. The brilliance of *Rogues* is that reason is not avoided in the aporia of democracy. But the aporetic non-sovereignty of reason – spirit – *is* avoided. Indeed, Derrida has always sought to protect spirit from itself as its own truth, fearing this closure, this self-knowing, as unacceptable. Derrida does not believe that absolute spirit can think radical alterity without engorging it into self-knowing, and therefore he needs to keep alive the possibility of the to-come that absolute spirit snuffs out. It is this presupposition of what is unacceptable for spirit that Derrida protects by way of *différance*. This is the unacknowledged mastery that grounds Derrida's critique of sovereignty.

In fact, the problem of mastery is not just the opposite of what Derrida understands it to be. It is in its triadic structure of opposition *and* identity that spirit has an absolute vulnerability to its own sovereignty. In ruling out the education carried in and by the triadic 'and', *différance*, iteration, deconstruction, autoimmunity and now reason/*différance* have never been free to know and to comprehend how vulnerability is shaped in and by modern social relations.[17] Absolute spirit is absolutely vulnerable to its absolute sovereignty. But for Derrida to accept this, he would have to philosophize power more according to the master/slave phenomenology than his prejudgement of truth will allow him. This is why spirit must be avoided in *Rogues*. It comes too close to finding a reasonable dialectic of sovereignty and non-sovereignty in reason/*différance*. It threatens to open up the possibility of spirit being known and knowable as the autoimmunity of the weaker rational force in relation to itself as sovereignty. If rationalization and reasonableness appear not just as the form of transformation, but also as the content of transformation, then this allows transformation to know itself, and when transformation knows itself as its own form and content this is the *Aufhebung* of absolute spirit, free to know itself in its presuppositions and not by avoiding them.

There is, then, an unacknowledged mastery underpinning Derrida's critique of mastery. To return for a moment to the language of *Rogues, différance* has always been the Security Council of absolute spirit, protecting the latter from misunderstanding its autoimmunity as total, and also has always been the same misunderstanding that sees the truth of Hegelian *Aufhebung* as dogma. Like the Security Council, *différance* hides its own mastery within a rationalization of protection, a protection that is also autoimmune and harms that which is being protected. The Security Council of *différance* is the suicide of the reasonable, a self-harming that precisely opposes the voices of reason that can speak the hard truth that this protection (i.e. *dif-férance*) is keeping vulnerable non-sovereignty from itself, from its truth. There is a sense in which *différance* takes for itself emergency powers to suspend spirit so that it may not be allowed to become sovereign completion. It appears therefore to suspend spirit for spirit's own sake, knowing what is good for it. But as with all emergency powers, law is suspended in order to invoke the law of suspension. The truth of this autoimmunity is kept away from spirit according the law of suspension. As such the truth of this auto-immunity is exported beyond itself, exposing the positing in the suspension of spirit of what is other to spirit.

We have seen in earlier chapters that exporting otherness beyond its being known aporetically in and as the self is the manifestation of misrecog-nition as political reality, and as political power. Otherness as the to-come, as the undecideable, is an emergency measure to provide for a concept of otherness that *différance* believes spirit and modernity incapable of keeping safe from total assimilation and corruption. But this has been Derrida's point all along. Keeping the other safe in this way is suicidal. Derrida wants to see the weaker force take 'account of the incalculable so as to give an account of it, there where this appears impossible, so as to account for or reckon *with* it, that is to say, with the event of *what* or *who* comes' (2005: 159). Yet, in fact, the weaker force is being protected by *différance* precisely from giving an account of it as itself, that is, as the autoimmunity of rational freedom as spirit. Derrida in the final analysis, protects political complicity from being its own determinative concept of political mastery and vulnera-bility. *Différance* can be such a concept, but not while it exiles the educative and formative content of absolute spirit from the comprehension of this concept.[18]

This brings us, then, to the different notions of transformation that Derrida and Hegel work with. When *différance* is related to a concept of rea-son that is defined by undecideability, what remains is a suspension lacking the transformative capacity that it seeks. Derrida's notion of transformative aporetic philosophical education – iteration alters: something new takes place – is left without the resources to know how to know what this altera-tion is. Doubling, *Glas*, autoimmunity and suspension are therefore not alteration at all. They never learn about learning and as such they are a repetition of the same education, a repetition of the emergency powers that suspends the truth of education for the sake for education. *Différance*, refused self-determination, never transforms because it is never trans-formed. What *différance* will never grant is the suspending of its suspension such that it might learn and therein transform itself. 'Iteration alters'

(Derrida, 1988: 40) is therefore only an intrigue. If transformation is by a reason/*différance* that contradicts itself then reason/*différance* is the dialectic of enlightenment. If it is by repentance then reason/*différance* is spirit. And if vulnerable non-sovereignty is 'a completely different story', how is this possible without the alteration of ipseity and *différance*, without, that is, an *Aufhebung* that is determined from within their own autoimmunity, and not avoided behind the autoimmunity of everything else? Even in his dramatic (re)turn to reason Derrida is still part of the emergency government charged with saving reason literally from itself. The result of this fear of self-completion is that in everything, save that of reason as spirit, Derrida identifies the government of the self in the definition of the other. The aporia of reason as spirit is denied this implication of itself in the other because it is denied the implication of itself as other to itself. Even the weaker force that acts without sovereignty has sovereignty in the weakness. But the *kind* of sovereignty it has, this is what remains for philosophy to comprehend in and of itself. This comprehension, spoken of by Derrida now as reason, requires reason to know itself in the otherness that determines it. Such a comprehension has all along been the *telos* of education in Hegel.

Fear of sovereignty

In conclusion, then, Derrida's philosophy remains one of the greatest adventures of absolute spirit and its misrecognition of itself in modern times. But it is his lack of faith in this misrecognition that returns his philosophy to him without ever having comprehended its own truth. Believing absolute spirit incapable of holding truth safe from the totality of difference-opposition, and believing it truthful *that he should do so*, he legislates against the autoimmunity of modern freedom believing himself to be legislating for it, for its possibility. He suspends freedom because he does not believe it is formative and re-formative of itself in the present. He thus avoids the totality of *Aufhebung*, a totality that we have seen in an earlier chapter[19] consists in *revolution* and *re-formation*, that is, in the circle of its comprehension and in the aporia of the comprehension of its circling. Thus, Hegel says, 'the tremendous difference in the world-historical situation is whether men are only implicitly [potentially] free or whether they know that it is their fundamental truth, nature, or vocation, to live as free [actual] individuals' (Hegel, 1987: 75). Hegel's *Aufhebung* accepts this total complicity in the social relations of mastery, that is, in abstract bourgeois social relations and the domination of abstract reason, in a way that the weaker force of non-sovereignty is denied in Derrida. What is required is for philosophy to retrieve the revolution and re-formation of reason within this, its own autoimmunity, and this means accepting culpability within the stronger force in a way that Derrida, for fear of sovereignty, does not do. As we have seen in earlier chapters, the export of fear is precisely the ground of modern sovereignty.

The real differences between Derrida and Hegel regarding aporetic philosophical education, then, become especially sharp in the political implications of their respective notions. In Derrida, we have to observe a lack of *total* complicity within his philosophy of complicity. It might amuse, I suppose, to be criticising Derrida for not being as open to the contradictions of totality as Hegel. At those moments when the otherness of *différance* could have come to know itself not merely as dogma but also as its own transformative form and content, Derrida seems to suffer a crisis of nerve, and he retreats to the presupposition that truth must not contain its own otherness as its education. We saw above how in one such moment of crisis in *Glas* Derrida invoked the event, not just as the circle of circles but as the spiral that refuses completion. This is a very telling educational metaphor in Derrida. If education is merely the circle of the same then there appears here to be no possibility of change. Therefore the spiral is needed to illustrate alteration such that the same does not return to itself but develops. However, the aporia here is that if the circle returns to the same the I does not develop, and if the spiral turns without returning there is no I to comprehend itself within that development. The spiral is not the metaphor for open-ended education that it at first appears to be. The spiral's development must return if it is to know of this *as* education. The subject and substance of aporetic education and of the Hegelian *Aufhebung* is here, in the impossibility of an education that can return and develop being known as both return and development in the impossibility, that is, in and as learning.

To herald a pledge, a promise, an originary, an impossibility and an undecideability is to refuse mastery one last time, and each time. It is to see the domination practised by the *logos* in opposition, abstraction, contradiction, and negation, but it is also to avoid this political totality by positing truth as other without return and without self-determination. It is to know complicity as mastery but still to refuse to become master. The irony here is this. It is when Derrida refuses absolute mastery that he is most totally master whereas, in Hegel, it is because he accepts the totality of mastery that, as master, he *can* know alteration in iteration. This is the difference between the two modes of education in Derrida and Hegel. It is the master alone who can know of and be changed by his experience of his own autoimmunity. It is the nature of political complicity in modern bourgeois social relations that absolute vulnerability and non-sovereignty are already a political reality in the master and it is he who will also know this fragility as a formative experience. This, again, is education in Hegel.

This is not, then, a political experience imbued with a pledge from beyond. This is an experience of freedom, within freedom, by freedom. It is an experience of the truth of complicity in freedom and of freedom in complicity. This is a doubling that does not have the luxury of excess, and where even what remains is consumed by mastery. This appears hopeless and resigned until and unless they are experienced as having their truth within education. Education is never resigned or hopeless because re-forming is the truth of what education is, and in this case it re-forms how we understand both hopelessness and resignation. This re-forming of totality within totality is the hard philosophical lesson of modern social and political contingency, *and* it is where and how the absolute appears in these modern social relations. Hegelian *Aufhebung* does not avoid the experience of vulnerability having its own truth in the master as his spiritual education. But there is no alteration in an iteration that merely affirms itself as undecideable. The master is decided already. This is the political implication of modern philosophy. It is from here that philosophy must have already begun. Derrida does not *seek* to avoid this political totality. Indeed, it is his aim to avoid avoiding it. He says that to do philosophy is 'to project the greatest mastery over all the possible discourses of mastery and to renounce it. The two things go together . . . [it is] a modesty haunted by the devil' (1995: 140). He is right here. But modest mastery in *différance* is protected against because the master can immodestly control the definition of mastery by which he is to be judged. The weakness and vulnerability of the master, as the master/slave relation makes clear, is *in* his mastery, and the greater this recognition, the greater, too, the modesty.

I have tried to show in this chapter how Derrida's protection of philosophy from the absolute has distorted his understanding of the *Aufhebung* and of education in Hegel. Derrida's notion of transformative aporetic education precludes from itself the truth in education that Derrida seeks for *différance*, for deconstruction, for iteration and for autoimmunity. *Différance*, the effect of iteration, has always disavowed itself of any triadic structure by refusing its construction within and by negation. To refuse negation is to avoid 'the self who is other and the other who is not me'. It results, as we have seen, in Derrida exporting otherness beyond spirit in order to protect spirit from its dogmatic assimilation of otherness. It is this avoidance of the negative and self-otherness that has the result of transformation in Derrida being form without content, a dialectic of nihilism.[20] The result has been that commentators search for ways in which *différance* makes a difference. In the Derrida I have presented above, *différance* makes all the difference; it changes everything, *until* it is asked to state what this difference consists in, and then it has nothing to say. It has no voice which can speak of how we should understand the truth of this change, or, therefore, of this philosophical education. Derrida, ironically like many Hegelians, wants the transformative power of aporetic critique without the burden of the absolute. But transformative philosophical education without absolute spirit is only the illusion of education. Nothing changes unless we are being re-educated about what change in and by education actually means. It is to remain uneducated about all transformation because it is to remain uneducated about education by education. This re-education is the truth of education in Hegel, transformative of the thinker in being thought.

Absolute ambition

Finally, now, I return to Beardsworth's challenge that aporetic philosophy, Derridean or Hegelian, is too unambitious in terms of its scope for transformation. Perhaps there are two notions of ambition at work here. Derrida's ambition in the way I have presented him is concerned with keeping alive and open the truth to-come that lies suppressed in and by the dominance of difference-opposition. The educational strengths and weaknesses of this we have explored in this chapter. What, then, of the Hegelian *Aufhebung*? What is the scope of its ambition? It shares Derrida's concern to expose aporia in identity, and to find meaning in difference and otherness. But its view of its complicity within prevailing social relations is very different from Derrida and at the most fundamental level. Hegelian *Aufhebung* is the experience of the risk that is run in trying to think truthfully. It speaks of the preparedness to live and work with the groundlessness of its own reason. This is philosophy as the vocation to be true to itself. If this means that it appears unambitious as a force for social transformation, then so much the worse for versions of transformation that are less than true to themselves.[21] Part of education in Hegel means learning to mediate ambition as also actual.

The *Aufhebung* does work for the middle, and does so by not presupposing the truth of the work beyond the unavoidable social and political presuppositions that already ground it. Beardsworth is right to be concerned about the ways in which the diremption of the universal and the particular are being played out on a global scale between master and servant. I hope that the other chapters in this book have begun to illustrate the contribution that education in Hegel can make to these debates. The centre is precisely what needs to be thought. But we should be ever mindful of imposed middles that are less than comprehending of the conditions that predetermine middles as broken middles. This is not a lack of ambition. If anything, it is painfully too ambitious, recognizing its own groundlessness yet still risking truth within such an actuality. It is wrong to mistake Hegel's 'grey in grey' for an end of formative philosophy. As I hope previous chapters have shown, recollection is not passive, nor is it nostalgic. It is our knowing of philosophy as formative and it is itself re-formative of this knowing. This is where the centre can be thought, and this too is not an unambitious project.

Notes

1. I use spirit and *Geist* interchangeably in this chapter.

2. I should add here that in this chapter I am not concerned with Derrida's critique of the Hegelian *Aufhebung*, except as it pertains to the form and content of *Glas*. Indeed, I am trying to draw out from Derrida the presuppositions that ground his idea of transformative aporetic philosophy as he practises it in *Glas*, *Of Spirit* and *Rogues*. It could be said, however, that Derrida retrieves from the *Aufhebung* all that he takes to be transformative from all that is dogmatic, and that *différance* is therefore his own version of the *Aufhebung*. While I think this is true, it would need a different chapter to make this case, one that did attend to Derrida's comments, beyond *Glas*, on Hegel.

3. This is taken from an as yet unpublished essay by Richard entitled 'Responding to a Post-Script: Philosophy and its Futures' (2007). It replies to a reply I had made to his slightly earlier essay 'A Note to a Political Understanding of Love in our Global Age' (2006) which published by the E-Journal *Contretemps*. The whole exchange was to be published by *Contretemps* but sadly the Journal ceased publishing before this was possible.

4. Derrida's italics.

5. Derrida's italics.

6. 'To relieve' is how Derrida's term *relever* in *Glas* – itself Derrida's translation of *Aufheben* – is translated in the English version of *Glas*. As I noted above in footnote 2 I have not extended this chapter to include Derrida's comments on the *Aufhebung* except as they constitute *Glas*.

7. This turn to the event in *Glas* is unjustified within or without the totality of difference-opposition. This Heideggerian move is an example of the presuppositions of the absolute that ground Derrida's critique of absolute knowing. This will become clearer in what follows.

8. From Hegel, (1988: 327).

9. Note here I am juxtaposing the end of *Glas* and the beginning.

[10] But not, as noted above, with the turn to the event.

[11] This is expressed by Löwith to Jaspers who, after hearing Heidegger's lecture on Hölderlin, 2 April 1936, sees this as the reason for Heidegger linking poetry to the swastika (Ott, 1994: 133).

[12] The context of this omission in *Introduction to Metaphysics* is important here. Heidegger is arguing that spirit has degenerated into mere cleverness, which itself becomes a tool, a value, and a political propaganda. Against this Heidegger commends 'a spiritual power which originally unites and engages, assigns, obliges' (*Of Spirit*: 65, *Introduction to Metaphysics*: 48; the translation of Derrida's translation is used here) and it is here that he chooses to illustrate this spiritual power by quoting from his own Rectoral Address but dropping the inverted commas around the first spirit. Thus we get 'spirit ['spirit' in the original] is neither empty sagacity, nor the gratuitous game of joking, nor the unlimited work of analysis of the understanding, nor even the reason of the world, but spirit [without inverted commas in the original] is the being-resolved [*Entschlossenheit*] to the essence of Being, of a resolution which accords with the tone of the origin and which is knowledge' (Derrida, 1987: 67). In addition, the chapter in *Introduction to Metaphysics* then proceeds to assign the originarity of this spiritual *Dasein* as within 'the absolute privilege of the German language' (1987: 68).

[13] Simon Critchley, for example, argues that it does. By granting the priority of the originary pledge or the promise that is affirmed, then, in the question and in opposition, this opens 'the ultimately *ethical* orientation of *Of Spirit*' (Wood, 1993: 95). If Hegel's anti-erection seeds virility against pressure, then Derrida's 'inversion or reversal' (1993: 96) of the question in effect puts the lead in Hegel's pencil (as it were). This new priority for Critchley is the Levinasian Other, a dimension of alterity and transcendence. Here, for holocaust we can read 'ethics of deconstruction'. Further, for Critchley, the footnote signals Derrida's 'departure' (1993: 95) from what he calls 'the repetitive order of commentary' (1993: 95) in *Of Spirit*. This departure needs to be understood as affirming the 'unconditioned duty' (1993: 94) that underpins deconstruction, that is, its 'ethical and political responsibility' (1993: 94). At root here, for Critchley, Derrida practises in deconstruction an 'undecideability' (1993: 94), a 'suspension of choice or decision between two alternatives, a suspension provoked in, as and through a practice of double reading' (1993: 94). See also Wood, 1993: 1.

[14] It is interesting here to note that this could well be a description of recollection, of the grey in grey. It is important then to bear in mind that there is no loss here for Derrida, no negation, and therefore nothing to be recalled from loss. The return is *différance*, not recollection; it is remarkable, but not self-(re-)formative.

[15] Derrida has always been mindful to remind his readers that he has never eschewed reason in his philosophy.

[16] It is interesting to note the mutuality of fear and risk achieved here in the policy of mutually assured destruction (MAD), but this mutuality still represents only a mutual export of fear. It is not the way that fear and vulnerability in the double negation of self and of self as other speaks its educational truth. MAD, because it is mutual, is not open to learning of fear as the self who is other and the other who is *not* this self. Learning is in the lack of mutuality; this is the real double negative of education in Hegel, a learning that MAD closes off from itself. MAD is

fear is stasis; this is its madness. But from Derrida's point of view it was perhaps safer for the world than less explicit autoimmunity.

[17] I have said more on the speculative and educative significance of this 'and' in an earlier work, *Philosophy's Higher Education*, (2004) chapter 6.

[18] I note here that Gillian Rose has stated that *différance*, comprehended speculatively, could have been the unity and difference of identity and difference (Rose, 1984: 139).

[19] see above, Chapter 1.

[20] See Gillian Rose's *Dialectic of Nihilism* (1984).

[21] At times in writing this chapter I have been struck by the thought that it might appear somewhat decadent to be arguing over whose version of vulnerable non-sovereignty is the right one. But, this too must be risked.

Chapter 5

Education in Hegel in Levinas

Introduction

Howard Caygill has recently said of Levinas that his 'anti-Hegelian operation is less the overcoming of Hegelian dialectic than its deflation' (Caygill,
2002: 53). In this chapter I want to reflate the Hegelian in Levinas or, more
accurately, to show how education in Hegel in Levinas in fact reflates itself
through the eternal return of presuppositions as oppositions. The chapter
is divided into three main sections. The first section looks at how Levinas
deflates the Hegelian dialectic in *Totality and Infinity* and *Otherwise than
Being*, with particular attention paid to three forms of education found
there, namely teaching, philosophy and study. The second section watches
the reflation of Levinas's anti-Hegelian operation in some of the poignant
and telling criticisms offered by Caygill. This reflation comes about by way
of the aporias that mediate Levinas's ethics, and for Caygill this is most
apparent in the oppositions of war and peace, and state and religion. The
final section reads this reflation as education in Hegel. It concentrates on
how the relation of state and religion, the notion of alterity, and the positing of error in philosophy are re-formed in such learning.

PART A

Deflating Hegel

Following Caygill's line of argument, Levinas's deflation of the Hegelian
dialectic amounts to emptying the system of the movement associated with
negation, mediation, contradiction and *Aufhebung*. Within such movement
Levinas finds only a repetition of the same from which no new result
emerges. As such, the Hegelian dialectic is emptied of the form and content
that represent its presupposition that nothingness can be determinate, can
be known. Against this, Levinas argues for a fundamental non-grounding of

the I in the isolation of anonymous being, in the insomnia of the *il y a* that is the 'horror, trembling, and vertigo, perturbation of the I that does not coincide with itself' (1969: 143). Within this trembling a revelation regarding alterity is possible for Levinas in the isolation of the existence of the I in the form of the immediate caress. This consolation, lacking any finite agenda, transports the I 'elsewhere' (2001: 93). It is the nature of this elsewhere and its presence in the totality of the same that comes to define Levinas's philosophical and ethical project, described in *Totality and Infinity* as instituting 'a relation with the infinity of being that exceeds the totality' (1969: 23).Where the Hegelian dialectic can sublate such nothingness into meaning, Levinas insists that this only posits endless representation of the same: a totality in which nothing is ever allowed to remain as an un-sublated or an un-sublatable other. Hegel's infinite, says Levinas, operates by 'excluding all multiplicity from it; he posits the infinite as the exclusion of every "other" that might maintain a relation with the infinite and thereby limit it' (1969: 196). This operation has meaning as time displayed in the history of philosophy and the philosophy of history; as subjectivity in substance; and as objective freedom in the rational political state. Each 'meaning' only repeats the totality of the same, and each is the paganism that sees God or ethics reduced to ontology.

Levinas's anti-Hegelian project is grounded then in the impossibility of knowing the other within the totality of the same. It will be an important part of the reflation of Hegel in Levinas to show how he judges the incommensurability of the same and the absolutely other. For example, in *Totality and Infinity* he says,

> the radical separation between the same and the other means precisely that it is impossible to place oneself outside of the correlation between the same and the other so as to record the correspondence or the non-correspondence of this going with this return. Otherwise the same and the other would be reunited under one gaze, and the absolute distance that separates them filled in. (1969: 36)

However, in judging that the same and the other are known as incommensurable Levinas posits for himself the very position that he deems impossible and illegitimate.[1] As we will see, mediation is already present in the assertions that Levinas makes for the difference between the same and the other, and as we will also see, the ground of this positing is of philosophy as error. Reflating positing retrieves the negative from within Levinas and returns him to education in Hegel. But this is not the Hegel found in

Levinas who 'posits the infinite as the exclusion of every "other" that might maintain a relation with the infinite and thereby limit it' (1969: 196). That Hegel, the one Levinas opposes, does not take account of education in Hegel as we are presenting it. This will become clear later, but preceding this we need to spend a little time exploring some of the key terms that constitute Levinasian ethics in *Totality and Infinity* and *Otherwise than Being*.

Totality and Infinity

In *Totality and Infinity* (1969) Levinas argues for three modes of non-Hegelian subjectivity that are interrupted by the absolutely Other.[2] Each is a form of desire, and each exposes the human subject to a fundamental vulnerability that exceeds the totality of the same. The interior life is both a happiness at having needs that can be satisfied – where, through taking in content it becomes content-ed – and a fragility at the uncertainty of attaining this content(ment) in the future. Time, however, expresses the vulnerability that needs cannot be certain to be satisfied in the future, and exposes the plenitude of enjoyment to 'the unknown that lurks in the very element it enjoys' (1969: 144). In doing so, time breaks up the totality of subjectivity and forces it beyond itself into relation with an alterity that cannot be assimilated. This vulnerability is consoled by the welcome that is 'in the gentleness of the feminine face' (1969: 150), a welcome that speaks to and of something other than the I.[3] The hospitality offered to vulnerability is the possibility of 'the transcendent relationship with the Other' (1996: 155).

The second mode of this vulnerability is expressed in property. In the interiority hollowed out by enjoyment there is formed a heteronomy 'that incites to another destiny' (1969: 149). The paganism of enjoyment is possession which, compared and quantified, is property. But the approach of the stranger calls into question 'my joyous possession of the world' (1969: 76) and this disquietude again breaches the totality of the ego. Here the relation to the Other is in the need to give or refuse to give what I have to the stranger. Thus, as the feminine graces the welcome that is the home, so generosity graces private property with the Other, and is therein the abolition of inalienable property rights.

The final example of the ambivalence of totality is expressed in Levinas's conception of metaphysical desire that 'tends towards *something else entirely*, toward the *absolutely other*' (1969: 33). '"The true life is absent." But we are in the world. Metaphysics arises and is maintained in this alibi' (1969: 33). Metaphysics breaches the satisfaction of man with himself with a desire that cannot be satisfied. This vulnerability, this *il y a*, draws beyond the I to 'the alterity of the Other and of the Most-High' (1969: 34), and it is present in the metaphysical import of the face-to-face.

These three breaches of totality by the welcome, by generosity and by the face-to-face speak against Hegelian negation and mediation. These latter oppose and sublate what is Other, whereas the former remain vulnerable in 'a non-allergic relation with alterity' (1969: 47). Levinas believes that this non-allergic relation remains open to God while the Hegelian operation closes it down. It is part of Levinas's argument here that desire is totality and infinity in a way that mediation cannot sustain. As such, the epiphany of the face-to-face relation is wholly Other and unassimilable, and contests its ability to be murdered by the same. This contestation and this epiphany are the stranger, the destitute, the widow and the orphan. This epiphany cannot be represented, for the same cannot think it. Its impossibility exhausts all the resources that the same can call upon to represent the Other, and exceeds them. It is the language of God, and on earth this language speaks as ethics and justice. It precedes thought and consciousness and breaches their totality by this precedence. 'A God invisible means not only a God unimaginable, but a God accessible in justice. Ethics is the spiritual optics' (1969: 78).

One can understand why Levinasian ethics has proved so attractive to a form of Western thinking that is trying to mediate its power in and over the world. For the view that the philosophical tradition of self-conscious reason has failed to protect the world from the horrors of war and from the Holocaust in particular, Levinas offers something absolutely beyond rational self-consciousness. In the loneliness and isolation of bare existence he finds God as the absolutely Other who is present in our vulnerability. Not in thought but in the physicality of the face, this truth is communicated to us as gentleness, as generosity and as the welcome. Levinas offers here an ethics that transcends the sovereignty of the rational I that is allergic to otherness, and an ethics that protects all that is best in human existence, that is, the truth that exists in our caring for others. He reconciles the transcendent with the deconstruction of absolutist philosophy and offers truth that is other than dogma, than imperialism, and than totality. In sum, he offers goodness without mediation, a face-to-face ethical relation 'maintained without violence [and] in peace' (1969: 197), maintained, that is, not in negation and return but in revelation. Negation 'remains within the totality' (1969: 209) whereas God exceeds this totality. As such, 'war presupposes peace' (1969: 199) because peace is the presence of God in the nakedness of the face before its being clothed in social relations. We will return to the theme of war and peace in Levinas below.

Already here there are themes that characterize education in Hegel, most importantly perhaps, that of vulnerability. In *Totality and Infinity* the I is vulnerable to himself as desire; he is vulnerable to the gaze of the other who breaches the I; he is vulnerable to the sovereignty in his property; and he is vulnerable to the truth of this vulnerability as metaphysics. In education in Hegel, however, the I is vulnerable to himself as his own other; he is vulnerable to the other who, even as other, is not the same other as he is to himself; and he is vulnerable to the truth of the relation of the two vulnerabilities, a truth he knows in education. But from our account of *Totality and Infinity* it is clear that Levinas sees himself addressing these themes in ways very different from Hegel.

Otherwise than Being

We turn now to some of the ways in which Levinas develops these themes in *Otherwise than Being*. This text continues Levinas's anti-Hegelian operation but there is an enforced change of emphasis due to the introduction of the third party to the relation of self and other. This complicates significantly the metaphysics of the social relation described in *Totality and Infinity*. Levinas employs terms in *Otherwise than Being* that move his thought on from that in the earlier text. Prior to the war of allergic egoisms there is now a relation of proximity, an originary ethical disinterestedness where responsibility of one for the other inverts the ego by substituting itself for the other who approaches. For Levinas, this is a different kind of subjectivity altogether from essence for it is where the 'Here I am' is hostage to and for the care of the other. It is found in the relation between 'saying' and the 'said'. Proximity, as originary ethics, is a saying that is beyond essence, beyond the dialogue that occurs between two people. The saying is therefore above the said in which the former is thematized, conceptualized and cognized. However, the latter is absolutely necessary as the 'lived time' (1998: 37) in which phenomena appear. While saying lies beyond essence as proximity and responsibility, the said exposes entities as phenomena and exhibits them around the subject–object relation. Synchronization is this assembling of entities in the totality of the present by the same, synchronized, that is, 'into a time that is recallable, and becomes a theme' (1998: 37). As such, says Levinas, 'the subordination of the saying to the said, to the linguistic system and to ontology, is the price that manifestation demands' (1998: 6). Saying, in being said, is 'a betrayal' (1998: 6), and further, it makes the otherwise than being, in this case saying, appear to be 'an event of being' (1998: 6).

Equally, proximity for Levinas is the primary form of sensibility, and cognition is only secondary to this. Proximity disturbs cognition and therefore essence in a way similar to the unrest seen above in *Totality and Infinity*. This disturbance is a 'coring out' (1998: 64), a murmur that is 'the non-coinciding of the ego with itself, restlessness, insomnia, beyond what is found again in the present' (1998: 64). This break up of the totality of essence is variously described by Levinas as the signifyingness of signification, illeity, and diachrony, in addition to proximity and substitution. They are, in sum, 'a tearing away of bread from the mouth that tastes it, to give it to the other' (1998: 64) and they are registered as physical sensations prior to their synchronization. Also similar to the relation of enjoyment and trauma in *Totality and Infinity* is the idea in *Otherwise than Being* that sensibility and suffering have no sense unless they are relative to the enjoyment which they tear apart. Sensibility is the pain of giving, for giving has a meaning 'only as a being torn from the complacency in oneself characteristic of enjoyment' (1998: 74). Proximity has meaning, says Levinas, 'only among beings of flesh and blood' (1998: 74). Substitution is material and real; it is not ideal.

How, then, within this totality, does Levinas conceive of the possibility of 'a break out of essence?'(1998: 8). This question focuses on the conditions of possibility for temporalization. Beyond temporalization with its return of the same, 'there must be signalled a lapse of time that does not return, a diachrony refractory to all synchronization, a transcending diachrony' (1998: 9). The lapse of time that transcends synchronization is the signification that is carried in saying, that is, the signification not of what is said but by the responsibility embodied in the approach of the neighbour. Here subjectivity becomes the signifyingness of signification; not a negation of subjectivity but more an overpowering of essence by the prior obligation of proximity to the other. This disinterestedness Levinas calls 'passivity' (1998: 49). Illeity is the term used for the ambiguity of the infinite that transcends synchronization yet requires that synchronization in order to exceed it. Illeity here is substitution of one for another: it is giving. It is, again, the 'tearing away of bread from the mouth that tastes it, to give it to the other' (1998: 64). This substitution of essence for illeity is the ambiguity beyond I or Thou. It is where 'I am inspired' (1998: 114).

If substitution is the signifyingness of the signification that bears responsibility for the other, and exceeds the limits of essence, diachrony is the anachronism of that excess. It is where saying is anachronism. As the-one-for-the-other is the signifyingness of the signification of the break-up of essence, so, diachrony is now revealed as immemorial time within temporalization, or within the present. Diachrony is the signifyingness of the signification of the lapse of time wherein the sovereignty of the totality of memory is exceeded. 'I am ordered toward the face of the other' (1998: 11) in the transcendence of time immemorial.

As with *Totality and Infinity* there are themes here that resonate with education in Hegel. Proximity is the vulnerability of an ego or a subject to the other who approaches, and illeity retains the ambiguity of vulnerability in looking to totality (as synchronization) and infinity (its excess, its otherwise than being) at the 'same' (divine and earthly) time. We will return to *Otherwise than Being* and to some of these themes below.

It is often not commented upon that education stands at the centre of Levinasian ethics. Education is explicit in *Totality and Infinity* but rather more implicit in *Otherwise than Being*. We will now explore three ways in which education is presented by Levinas: as teaching, as philosophy and as study.

Teaching

If the relation of totality and infinity is neither concept nor representation nor any act of assimilation by knowledge in the totality, how is this epiphany structured? Levinas's answer to this is *teaching* which he affirms in *Totality and Infinity* as the relation that binds the vulnerability of totality to the vulnerability that is infinity.

The breaches of totality are found within time, property and desire. These breaches form a relation with the Infinite that is, as Levinas says, 'non-allergic' (1969: 51). The special quality of this relation is that it is expressed in the face and commands a response of welcome, generosity and metaphysics. This command, which is not experienced as object or subject, is what Levinas refers to as 'a teaching' (1969: 51). From the other is received more than the I. To receive is both a breach of totality and a teaching therein about infinity. The primacy of teaching is the 'primacy of an irreducible structure upon which all other structures rest' (1969: 79). It is, in this sense, part of 'the marvel of creation' (1969: 89) which creates 'a being capable of receiving a revelation, learning that it is created, and putting itself in question' (1969: 89). As such, says Levinas, 'the miracle of creation lies in creating a moral being' (1969: 89) or a being who from his isolation is open to being taught about his creation through the absolutely Other. It is in this teachability, characteristic of the created moral being, that justice comes to be known.

Levinas also argues that teaching is contained in the transitivity of the face and the feminine. They are capable of the transitivity from having to giving, a transitivity that knows itself as education. The face and the feminine signify the signifyingness of this educational movement. As such, they are not just teaching; they are also learning, and part of their teaching is that one learns to be teachable. Becoming teachable, in Levinas, is becoming responsible. Levinas is clear, however, that teaching must not be seen as a middle term. 'Western philosophy,' he says, 'has most often been an ontology: a reduction of the other to the same by interposition of a middle and neutral term that ensures the comprehension of being' (1969: 43). Teaching in Levinas avoids this reduction to the same by arguing that teaching is not a neutral conjoining of subject and object in (free) cognition. Rather, teaching is the break up of all such reconciliations and all such illusions of freedom and knowledge. Teaching is in the trauma of the loss of the latter and teaches that alterity cannot be reduced to such freedom and knowledge.

Teaching in *Totality and Infinity* is thus required to carry the weight of infinity exceeding totality. As we saw above, Levinas introduces the idea around the non-allergic relation to the Other, that is, the ethical relation. It is the calling of the I beyond itself and its view of itself as an essence, to the relation with the Other who 'approaches me not from the outside but from above' (1969: 171). Thought can thematize everything that is exterior to it and assimilate it into the same; but it cannot assimilate the teacher who makes thematization possible. This transcendence is in the unassimilable face of the Other. Teaching is what is received from this height; it is the face of the Master. Levinas continues here,

> this voice coming from another shore teaches transcendence itself. Teaching signifies the whole infinity of exteriority. And the whole infinity of exteriority is not first produced, to then teach: teaching is its very production. The first teaching teaches this very height, tantamount to its exteriority, the ethical . . . The Other is not another freedom as arbitrary as my own, in which case it would traverse the infinity that separates me from him and enter under the same concept. His alterity is manifested in a mastery that does not conquer but teaches. Teaching is not a species of a genus called domination, a hegemony at work within a totality, but is the presence of infinity breaking the closed circle of totality. (1969: 171)

Teaching, then, is not just about God; it is the truth of God expressed in the face. It is not merely a conceptual knowledge; it is the breach of the totality of concepts. Its education is radical; its expression teaches that the infinite *requires* the separated and isolated being in order that the infinite can breach the totality in its teaching. Without the atheism of the ego, there would be no teaching of the absolutely Other. The miracle of creation is that it creates in such a way that it can be revealed, present but absent. Teaching is this revelation. 'The contradiction between the free interiority and the exteriority that should limit it is reconciled in the man open to teaching' (1969: 180).

Additionally, Levinas holds that because teaching comes from beyond totality it is a 'non-violent transitivity' (1969: 51). The importance here of the notion of transitivity cannot be underestimated in Levinas's anti-Hegelian operation. Signification, expression, infinity, transcendence, the ethical, the face in Levinas all claim some kind of transitive quality in which what they do is also what they are. In transitivity, then, Levinas seeks to evade the dualism of theory and practice at the level of the transcendent. If the dualism *did* persist, then the 'epiphany of the face' (1969: 51), for example, would split into the totality of immediacy and its representation. Thus, teaching in Levinas is 'the coinciding of the revealer and the revealed in the face' (1969: 67). It is not, as it were, under a category, and first of all it teaches this teaching itself, by virtue of which alone it can teach. It is the primacy of the ethical. It effectuates the welcome of the other and therefore 'expresses a simultaneity of activity and passivity' (1969: 89) which places the relation with the other outside of the dichotomies of the *a priori* and the *a posteriori*. Teaching, then, is the non-conceptual relation of totality and infinity. But by its very nature it is in contact with the conceptualizations of totality, for it is the truth of their vulnerability to becoming breached. Despite the emphasis that is sometimes placed only on the exteriority of infinity, teaching retains the ambivalence of being infinity in relation to totality. If there is no relation, there is no teaching.[4]

In addition, teaching in Levinas has to be distinguished from the teacher/student relation restricted within totality. Theirs is a totality defined by freedom and lack of freedom, whereas the transitivity of teaching, of infinity in the face-to-face, 'leaves the plane of economy and labour' (1969: 181). The temporal teacher and student represent teaching as the war of totality in which knowledge is possession and autonomy. Teaching in the epiphany of the face, however, is described in *Totality and Infinity* as 'peace' (1969: 203). The face – teaching – does not offend my freedom, 'it calls it to responsibility' (1969: 203), and is a peace that 'maintains the plurality of the same and the other' (1969: 203). This is another occasion where Levinas grants priority to peace over war, finding here 'the first rational teaching, the condition for all teaching' (1969: 203).

Teaching is not explicitly pursued in *Otherwise than Being*, yet its transitivity is retained in the ways that signify the Other beyond the dichotomy of activity and passivity, that is, in the 'passivity of passivity' (1998: 143) which he also calls the glory of the Infinite. As such, education in *Otherwise than Being* is carried in the language of ethics by which the ego is commanded beyond itself. Justice is the most important conduit of divine education here, and we will explore justice a little later. Aside from justice, sincerity is one of the ways in which the *il y a* 'is identified with nothing but the very voice that states and delivers itself, the voice that signifies' (1998: 143). The scandal of sincerity, then, is 'the impossibility of being silent' (1998: 143).

Philosophy

A further way in which education is carried in *Otherwise than Being* is in philosophy. Much of Levinas's criticism of philosophy is part of an engagement with Hegel, Heidegger and Husserl. However, with a view to the educational in Levinas we will concentrate on the critical moment of scepticism within philosophy that he draws attention to and its import beyond essence in otherwise than being.

His most sustained commentary on philosophy in *Otherwise than Being* comes amid a host of questions he asks about whether philosophy is a reduction of otherwise than being to the same. For example, in chapter 5 he notes that some might say that

> the very discussion which we are at this moment elaborating about signification, diachrony and the transcendence of the approach beyond being, a discussion that means to be philosophy, is a thematizing, a synchronizing of terms, a recourse to systematic language, a constant use of the verb being. (1998: 155)

Levinas is dismissive of this kind of scepticism. Such objections, he says, are 'facile' (1998: 155). It has been the whole point of his treatise to show how 'everything is shown by indeed betraying its meaning' (1998: 156) and that when philosophy draws attention to this abuse, as Levinas has done, then this is precisely the abuse 'that justifies proximity itself [and] in which the Infinite comes to pass' (1998: 156). The contradiction of signification requires 'a second time' (1998: 156) to that of the immemorial, a time that Levinas calls 'reflection' (1998: 156), the time in which contradiction appears. Reflection is the time of the contestation of the meaning of significance but it is not the time of two simultaneous statements; it is the time 'between a statement and its conditions' (1998: 156). The contestation that this produces is self-consciousness. Self-consciousness here is the result of time interrupting eternity. As such, philosophy can only achieve an ambivalent status: it is the knowing of proximity and it is the undermining of that knowing, for in its betrayal is the immediacy *from which* philosophy arises. Thus philosophy can do no better than 'to conceive ambivalence' (1998: 162).

However, in this ambivalence there is 'the periodic return of scepticism and of its refutation' (1998: 167). Levinas sees scepticism as a refusal of synchronization, one that returns again and again and is insensitive to attempts to refute or totalize its return. As such, scepticism for Levinas has an important educational significance. It contests the synchrony of the same in such a relentless way that Levinas credits scepticism with being 'sensitive to the difference' (1998: 168) between saying and the said, and between the same and the other. Crucially here Levinas states that because of this sensibility, and because scepticism refuses to be assimilated as the negation that reabsorbs every difference into its own order of the same, 'scepticism in fact makes a difference' (1998: 168). The difference it makes is that because it returns it exceeds all absorption into the self-contradictory. This articulates how education in Levinas's philosophy is to be distinguished from education in Hegelian negation. The totalitarianism of the latter can refute scepticism in terms set by the negative, but it cannot totally refute it because scepticism 'returns' (1998: 168) in the face (as it were) of totality. Scepticism carries 'the trace of the saying' (1998: 168), a trace that because it does not appear within 'the logical scope of negation and affirmation' (1998: 168) is wholly underestimated by philosophy. This trace is an alternating movement which is 'without end and without continuity. [It] is a tradition' (1998: 169) and it renews itself as an 'excluded middle' (1998: 169).

Scepticism then is anti-Hegelian. But Caygill argues that this is not able to complete a rejection of Hegel, only its deflation. Levinas, he says, sustains the power of the negative while remaining vigilant 'not to endorse the negation of the negation' (2002: 54). Indeed, says Caygill, Levinas 'diverts negation into an iterative circuit of the eternal return of botched negations' (2002: 54). The substance of Caygill's claim, I believe, lies in the fact that education in Hegel is not characterized by allergy to otherness, nor is it able to totalize scepticism such that it makes no difference. Otherness and the return of scepticism, in education in Hegel, do not just trace a difference, they oppose themselves in the tracing. To say that this opposition is 'other' than the truth of otherness in scepticism is to separate its return, its dialectic, from itself. This is the protection from the negation of the negation that Caygill refers to. The deflation is grounded in positing the difference between 'other' in opposition and 'other' in the trace – which is a positing of the very concept of otherness that is presenting itself in its eternal moments. We might risk saying here that Hegel's absolute and Levinas's otherwise than being witness the same movement, they just differ in how open they are to learning of eternity from this eternal return. Hegel is open to learning that all judgements of the same and the other are grounded in a positing of the identity and non-identity of what otherness is. It is this positing that is used by Levinas as the criterion for judging what is and what is not Other. As education in Hegel has shown us in previous chapters, it is not just that otherness is posited here before the enquiry into what it is is carried out, although this remains the case in Levinas. When he judges such mediation as allergic to otherness it is a judgement based in precisely this positing. It is also the case that what is being judged as Other comes from the point of view of the life that already has death as other. The very concept of otherness hides the relation that determines it. We will return to this presently. This same risk in bringing Hegel and Levinas together here is also recognized in calling their relation to each other not one of mere opposition, but one of deflation and reflation. There is still opposition between totality and infinity and in otherwise than being, but the deflation and reflation of education in Hegel are the import of these oppositions in Levinas, that is, where scepticism falls to itself in the significance of its own eternal return.

Study

Caygill notes that in some of his Talmudic Commentaries Levinas articulates the State of Israel as 'bearing witness to the promise of a new kind of state' (2002: 167), a new form 'of the political that marks the transformation of the territorial nation-state' (2002: 175). The University – or a University of the Jewish State – offers Levinas an institution both universal and particular in and out of time. The University is to unite the Diaspora and the State of Israel in and as a prophetic politics. Caygill in his concluding *Afterword* looks to *study* as the 'equivocal blessing and danger of fire' (2002: 199). Reading the 'forgotten, ancient, difficult books' (2002: 200) substitutes for burnt offerings, while the life spent in the study of the former breathes life into the embers and provides both fire and light. Caygill notes that this 'blaze of the many readings that make up the Diaspora contrasts with the uniform light of philosophy, politics and the state'

(2002: 200). Study breaks up the totality of the same. Equally, at times for Levinas the fire is the inextinguishable flame of the transcendent which traverses history as suffering. This strange fire exceeds its temporal finitude by being the 'permanent horizon of marvel' (2002: 201). It is beyond 'the prudence of techniques; without calculation [and] without past' (2002: 202). This education is the strange fire that is kept apart from war or political struggle.

PART B

Reflation in aporia

In this section we begin the Hegelian reflation of Levinas's anti-Hegelian operation. In his book *Levinas and the Political*, Caygill has developed an aporetic critique of Levinas that reveals both an inescapable terror in Levinas's politics – a terror carried by war and peace – and, for Caygill, a sadness, perhaps even a pessimism, regarding the actuality of the modern political state.[5] As such, his analysis stands in stark contrast to those who see in Levinas an 'irreproachable ethical rigour' (2002: 1). He exposes aspects of Levinas's political judgement that are 'chilling' (2002: 1) in their 'unsentimental understanding of violence and power' (2002: 1). In this section I want to look at two themes that Caygill uses to illustrate how aporia and mediation reflate Levinas in ways that re-educate us regarding his ethics. The first theme is that of war and peace, and the second is religion and the state.

War and peace

That Caygill finds the theme of war and peace central to Levinas's work is not surprising once one recalls Levinas's own life. He witnessed the wars that followed the Russian revolution from his home in Lithuania and the Ukraine. He was a prisoner in World War II but lost members of his family to the Holocaust. He witnessed the foundation of the state of Israel and he was in France for the events of 1968. As such, Caygill concludes, Levinas's political philosophy 'is haunted by an unassimilable past of political horror and an unforeseeable future of political promise' (2002: 3). As a result, says Caygill, for Levinas 'it is irresponsible to speak of peace without war, or to imagine a peace that is but the cessation of war: war is inextricable from peace, violence is inextricable from ethics' (2002: 3).

War in Levinas is the war of ontology and totality which is waged against proximity and responsibility. Peace is the peace of ethics or of illeity which is waged against and of necessity within the totality of the same. The weapons of war are representation and essence; the weapons of peace are trauma and substitution. The work of justice, as Caygill says, is the between of ethics and ontology. It is the middle 'that opens the space for politics, but which also leaves the character of that space undecideable' (2002: 96).

In his discussion of *Totality and Infinity* Caygill notes how Levinas's concept of totality holds within itself the relation of war and peace. Totality as a concept in Levinas begins by encompassing Heideggerian ontology but by *Totality and Infinity* it refers to 'the entire history of Western philosophy' (2002: 94). Both share the imperative to extend their sovereignty over the whole of exteriority which Caygill calls 'the violent identification of totality and exteriority through war' (2002: 95), or war used to make the present a totality and the totality a present, or 'an objective order' (2002: 104; Levinas 1969: 21). On the other hand, they also share the disruption that, by definition, what seeks totality cannot be total. This 'intrinsic incompletion' (2002: 95), says Caygill, 'anachronistically disrupts its identity' (2002: 95), but it also means that war in the cause of totality is, at root, not only 'the permanent possibility of war' (2002: 105) but also meaningless self-destruction, 'sacrifice for the sake of sacrifice' (2002: 105). Thus Caygill finds an 'horrific phenomenology of war' (2002: 119) in Levinas where any opposition to war, for example, by eschatological politics, becomes 'a declaration of war by peace upon war' (2002: 107).[6] Such aporias are Caygill's reflation of the mediation that persists in Levinas.

Levinas begins *Totality and Infinity* by asking whether we are 'duped' by morality when it fails to see itself in war with peace. He ends by asking in what ways peace, the triumph of the Messianic which is ever deferred, can be present as politics, or as peace in war? Caygill argues here that the beginning and the end of *Totality and Infinity* in fact replay the difficulty of the middle between war and peace. At the beginning Levinas asks whether 'lucidity, the mind's openness upon the true, consist[s] in catching sight of the permanent possibility of war?' (1969: 21). At the end of the book the Messianic has acknowledged its own collaboration in this permanent possibility.

War and peace are also thematized in Levinas's later work, *Otherwise than Being*. Caygill argues here that *Totality and Infinity* solicits the ethical within ontology while *Otherwise than Being* seeks the 'ontological within the ethical' (2002: 96). The first chapter of the latter draws attention to the fact that essence, as *interest*, is the state of war in which egoisms struggle with one another 'each against all, in the multiplicity of allergic egoisms which are at war with one another' (1998: 4). Essence, says Levinas, is thus 'the extreme synchronism of war' (1998: 4). The remedy for such an allergy is not a 'rational peace' (1998: 4) for in reason interest becomes objectified as 'calculation, mediation [ ] politics [and] exchange and commerce' (1998: 4). As such, 'the mass remains permanent and interest remains. Transcendence is factitious and peace unstable. It does not resist interest' (1998: 5). It is in the disinterestedness of passivity that Levinas looks to find the peace that undoes all interest through substitution. Caygill observes that 'in the final sections of *Otherwise than Being*, Levinas searches for arguments that will link the ethical categories of proximity, substitution and responsibility with the order of ontology' (2002: 141). Thus *Otherwise than Being* ends as it and *Totality and Infinity* began: 'with war. But this is war – with all the ontological entailments that Levinas has taught us to see – now waged with a bad conscience. The otherwise than being is not otherwise than the war that Levinas has shown accompanies ontology' (2002: 143). These aporias reflate the contradictions of a totality that cannot avoid mediation by that which fails to exceed it.

Religion and the state

The relation of religion and the state in *Otherwise than Being* in a sense exceeds the relation of totality and infinity. In the earlier book, justice was the language of God, and was 'social' in the sense that the face-to-face is always a relation between egos and always an event of communication. But in *Otherwise than Being* this triadic relation can no longer be sustained against the problem posed by the third party.

The third party is other to the face-to-face or to proximity. In this case Levinas is clear that illeity has to recognize that its other in substitution is also other to another, that is, also in a relation of substitution to someone else. This recognition of the relation of substitution to a third party raises the question of how religion stands against the demands for calculated, rational and objectified universal justice? How, in other words, is prophetic justice to relate to state justice?

In addressing this Levinas distinguishes two violences. The first is the divine violence that defeats the ego in illeity. The ego is commanded here but not as a slave, for 'no one is a slave of the Good' (1998: 138). Divine violence accuses and redeems prior to any intentionality or will, just as the face in its destitution is both an accusation and an epiphany. The second violence is the interruption of substitution by the third man, the other to my neighbour. Yet this violence is latent in the first violence. If proximity only concerned the-one-for-the-other then, says Levinas, it would not have been troubled into consciousness, self-consciousness or a question. Proximity takes on a new meaning here. 'The third party introduces a contradiction in the saying whose signification before the other until then went in one direction' (1998: 157). This contradiction arouses the question 'what has justice to do with me?' a contradiction sustained in the relation of illeity and justice. It is here, however, that the possibility arises of judgements as to who is for or against those in proximity.

Caygill draws attention to the problems that are latent, and sometimes explicit in Levinas's construction of these two middles of illeity and justice. His concern, primarily, is that Levinas can be seen to defend a relation of responsibility between I and other while pitting this relation against the third party. This in effect means that the third party is not otherwise than being but *otherwise than other*. If justice is controlled by proximity there need be no rational order of justice. Additionally, proximity could wage 'just' war against a third party. This is what Caygill refers to when he talks of 'war waged with a bad conscience' (2002: 143).

There are times identified by Caygill when the antinomical relation of the two middles of illeity and justice is resolved against the third party, For example, he notes that in a 1968 interview Levinas chose silence – and, recall here, as we saw earlier, silence is not possible for sincerity – in response to a question about the State of Israel. Caygill remarks on the echoes of Heidegger's silence over the Holocaust in World War II. The point here is that when the state is seen as serving proximity against the third party Levinas is in danger of 'supporting injustice and forgetting the third for the sake of the Other – and thus indeed sacrificing Israel to the idol of the State of Israel' (2002: 166).

As we noted above, Levinas seeks to articulate the State of Israel as 'bearing witness to the promise of a new kind of state' (2002: 167). Now Caygill draws attention to the deeper antinomies of trying to do so, that is, of trying to discern a '"superposition" of messianic eschatology and political ontology' (2002: 170). This superposition forces terms such as 'particular universal' (2002: 170) which serve only to reflate mediation in Levinas. Caygill is critical of the way that Levinas, faced with the real antinomy of justice and the state of Israel, remains silent at the point of its greatest difficulty. Indeed, again from Levinas's Talmudic readings, Caygill argues that Levinas elides this difficulty of the (Hegelian) problem of universal and particular by giving priority to the prophetic – namely the Diaspora and the Talmud – over the concern for justice within the state and to its neighbours

who are excluded from proximity. Caygill concludes that 'Levinas's claim to
a right of silence regarding the actions of the State of Israel reneges on his
own political philosophy' (2002: 176).[7]

Caygill's deeply worrying conclusion on the ambivalences of the political
in Levinas is that at times Levinas does not hold the holy and the universal
apart but, in fact, joins them in a collusion of ethics (religion) and 'humanity' (the state) precisely *against* those third parties that interrupt the relation
of I and other. The third, in this case, says Caygill, is Asia in general and 'the
third Abrahamic religion – Islam' (2002: 183) in particular. As such there
remains an ambivalence in Levinas as to whether 'Islam is indeed part of
the holy history' (2002: 183), and rather less ambivalence in one essay in
1960, where Levinas refers to Asia as 'the yellow peril' (2002: 184). Caygill
concludes that this essay at least reveals an 'aspect of Levinas's thought that
arguably compromises many of his universalist ethical claims' (2002: 185).

Caygill goes on to show how Levinas argues for and against Islam in holy
history: how he both blamed and removed from blame the Arab world for
Auschwitz; but how, at crucial times, for example in discussing the issue of
the Palestinians – and in particular the massacres in the Palestinian refugee
camps of Sabra and Shatila – the ethical is left 'trailing behind the political'
(2002: 189). The prophetic, by having justice as other, can only ever be the
continuation of the political war by messianic means, a war clearly endorsed
by Levinas who, when interviewed about the massacres, responded by arguing that the violent third party, the Palestinians, forces the hand in defence
of the genuine face-to-face. Is this the same as saying that the Palestinian is
not other in substitution but rather other to substitution? Is it to say that the
third party is the enemy of alterity? Is it, in sum, to say that the prophetic
and the political must work with God on their side? Caygill says here that
Levinas's claim for the war against the third party to proximity is 'rigorously
consistent with his philosophy, which we have argued recognizes the inevi-
tability of war. To describe the other as enemy as this point is thus entirely
consistent with such a reading of Levinas's ethics' (2002: 192–93).

Caygill's concerns here begin to reflate the Hegelian dialectic that Levinas has sought all along to avoid. This reflation is the return of mediation.
It is not a return that is posited from outside of Levinas's thought but is a
return that is immanent within Levinas's anti-Hegelian operation. Caygill
hints at such a return when, in his discussion of the state as the middle in
Totality and Infinity, he notes that 'the repetition of the opposition of theory
and the concrete [up to and in *Totality and Infinity*] will prove increasingly
disruptive in Levinas's later thought, producing a split between Israel as a
"utopia of the human" and the violent internal and external politics of the
State of Israel' (2002: 115).[8]

PART C

Reflation as education

In this final section we will briefly discuss four aspects of education in Hegel as they pertain to the anti-Hegelianism of Levinas. The first three are in regard to the relation of religion and the state, alterity, and philosophical error. The final aspect concerns the educational imperative in Hegel.

State and religion

One of the most difficult propositions in Hegel is that 'religion and the foundation of the state are one and the same' (1984: 452). As such, the state and its laws 'are nothing else than religion manifesting itself in the relations of the actual world' (1956: 417). This statement requires to be comprehended not as an abstract assertion of identity, but as subsisting in education in Hegel. We have seen in other chapters how recollection has its own educational form and content in the learning of negation by that which is negated. Recollection here is the *Aufhebung* that knows its own nothingness. The implication of this is that consciousness already contains the actuality of the object that it seeks to comprehend. To know an enquiry structured in this way is to comprehend education in Hegel and, in particular, to comprehend the illusions that rule in the absence of such education. In seeking to understand the relation of state and religion this education in Hegel teaches us that our object is already present or actual in the form of the enquiry.

More important than any hermeneutical significance here is that the enquiry appears to take the 'natural' form of a relation of thought to its object. It is as this natural appearance that the relation of state and religion hides its own determinative role. Its influence is veiled by making the relation of thought to object appear completely transparent. But the transparency is precisely the form of its political and religious intervention. Thus, the relation of state and religion is not waiting passively to be discovered. It is already active in determining the terms of the enquiry. It is the failure to see transparency in the relation of thought to its object as illusion that fails also to understand how the relation of state and religion determines how we perceive reality. Reality is the victory of political determination as transparent and unseen. Actuality knows reality as illusion, but knows too that it is also illusion. Actuality is by its very nature held by this recollection that knows illusion (negates it) and remains illusion (the *Aufhebung*). The truth of education in Hegel is here: that only as learning, as education, can it hold the truth of negation as its own actuality.

This truth of education is easily avoided. When illusion contains truth as unknowable it hides itself within the critique of dogma, of the decideable and of the closure practised by the same. Equally, when illusion posits truth as objective and knowable it hides itself in the openness of non-foundational thought. It is the work of illusion, in this case the prior relation of state and religion, which is transparent and unseen, that defines truth and error as naturally incompatible. In Levinas, teaching, philosophy and study are responses to this natural opposition and even the claim made for them by Levinas as not oppositional but revelatory, is itself a claim grounded in the natural relation of totality and infinity. Education in Hegel exposes the natural here as political. It teaches that the relation of totality to infinity taken as one of closure and transcendence is a judgement grounded in and reproductive of the natural appearance in which the political hides. Illeity and justice repeat the same. This repetition of the illusions that constitute the relation of state and religion reflates the Hegelian in Levinas. The significance of this reflation and the ultimate difference between education in Levinas and education in Hegel is that God can be known in the illusions of the modern political state.

In recollection, then, we learn that what is actual is the modern form of the relation between religion and the state. The illusion of this relation as natural grounds our understanding of the nature of human transformative activity, of man and his object. Currently, this man is the sovereign property-owning bourgeois individual whose autonomy is complicit with the view of nature as object. This is the natural arena of modern life in which God and property, religion and the state are the one truth appearing separate from each other. This means that education in Hegel can find God in bourgeois social relations, but not in a religion that holds to an inwardness separate from modern law and freedom. God in (and as) education in Hegel is in actual social and political life, and includes the appearance of inwardness. To separate them, let us say, into the converted and the heathen, is to miss altogether how God is known in modernity.

The separation of state and religion is therefore not characterized as the feudal unhappy consciousness, although as we will see in the final chapter below this remains a constitutive moment of modern subjectivity. Rather, this separation is the freedom of subjectivity in universal property rights. It is education in Hegel, and in particular its learning of the truth of such illusions, that provides for a critique of universal property rights that remembers that this learning is the *Aufhebung* and not an overcoming. In this is the essential openness of philosophical critique to its being compromised by its own conditions of possibility. This is why it cannot be dogma.

One final point here. The non-dogmatic education regarding truth in social relations means that education in Hegel is open to the truth of other forms of the relation between state and religion. This pertains to the question of the third party, the other to the relation of state and religion. The state that is open to being other than itself, that knows itself in illusion, is also in relation to another state. Here, the state is already other to itself and the other state is not it. Here too is world spirit in education in Hegel, for it is the state that knows how to find itself in the other state *because* the other state is other to it. Nation can speak unto nation as it speaks unto itself. In the negation of the modern state by itself and in relation to its other it has a universal language, the language of the negation of the negation, that is, of their truth as relation in education. Vulnerability here is not weakness, but rather the strength gained in the truth of vulnerability. It is not so much that this truth can change the world, but rather that it changes it all the time, but only more or less recognized for what it is.

Alterity in education in Hegel

We have already seen in previous chapters that education in Hegel is a philosophy of self and other[9]. This can now be revisited in relation to the face-to-face in Levinas. The reflation of his anti-Hegelian operation means that the Hegelian notion of alterity is present in Levinas's thinking but it is eschewed from it within a natural appearance of the same opposed to the Other. As we noted above, this prejudgement in Levinas posits the relation of the same and Other even before the enquiry into them has begun. When God is cast beyond the same he is cast also beyond social relations. But this is an activity *of* social relations, themselves already a shape of the knowing or not knowing of God. The prior mediation of self and Other is not optional here. As such, one of the ways that education in Hegel differs from Levinas is in the recognition of a lack of mastery over mediation. Positing an absolute alterity is just such an act of mastery over mediation. The truth in proximity is therefore a truth un-re-formed in and by the mediation of this mastery over mediation. Positing a beyond of political totality is already the mediation by politics and religion of each other. This comes down, as so often in education in Hegel, to a question of complicity. The critique of totality is always a self-critique. This is why learning, and neither a notion of overcoming nor of a beyond, is the truth of this critique.

Complicity within the relation of state and religion educates us regarding Levinas's notion of the face-to-face. In education in Hegel there is no face-to-face as Levinas describes it. The face-to-face in education in Hegel is of life and death. It is as death in life that life is lived learning of itself as absolute vulnerability. But the face-to-face of life and death is relieved in Levinas's notion of the face-to-face, relieved that is, in that the face already has death as other, as the other face. Levinas's face-to-face does not recognize its predetermined political actuality. It does not, and this says the same thing, comprehend how the face-to-face is already a formation of state and religion which is itself already a formation of life and death. Against Levinas, then, education in Hegel teaches here that the *il y a* and the transcendent are not the trembling and the epiphany of the absolute that Levinas claims. In fact they relieve the face from having to recognize in itself the reproduction of prevailing social and political relations. The relief means that the natural appearance of the I as life that has death as other remains unchallenged. It is education in Hegel that retrieves death for the I as a critique of the natural political relations of the face-to-face. This educates the face that the one face is already other to itself and that the other face, the face that faces it, is not it. We have seen what happens when Levinas exports the face-to-face of life and death into a totality of the same; the third party returns as the mediation carried by death, and can be accommodated or refused according to the whim of God in proximity.

Education in Hegel, then, offers a very different account of self, other and the third party than is found in illeity and justice in Levinas. Illeity is the Otherness of self and other, and justice is the otherness of self and other. We must ask of Levinas, what prejudgement of truth is it that can be sure that Otherness and otherness are not the one truth, or that they are other to each other?[10] Such a presupposition is grounded in the positing of truth as other to its being known or, as we will see in a moment, as error. This positing is, as we saw above, merely an unchallenged reproduction of the natural appearance of state and religion. Levinas's ethics is grounded in such an appearance. It is what leads him to judge that Otherness and otherness are not the same. But education in Hegel teaches that this positing already carries within it a historically specific shape of the relation of state and religion. Taken as a neutral and obvious judgement that God and society cannot be the same, it is in fact the modern shape of their relation parading as if the relation were yet to be established. Seen in this way, the difference between Otherness and otherness is really a philosophical education regarding the politics of their appearance as different. This does not mean that suddenly they are reconciled. But it does mean that we learn the truth of their separation as our own political actuality.

Contrary to Levinas's misrecognition of self, other and third party, illeity and justice can be re-formed into education in Hegel as 'I am already other and the other is not me'. I am already other means my relation to myself is one of absolute vulnerability. Equally, the other as not me means that my vulnerability is not returned to me as my own by my finding otherness in an other. There is no mutual recognition here. The opposite is the case. Even my vulnerability is other than the other. But nor is there justification for refusing my having vulnerability as the actual truth of myself, proved, as it were, precisely because it is not reconciled by finding the same in the other. This is the truth of otherness in the negation of the negation, that is, where otherness is absolutely unable to know itself. Levinas, ruling out the possibility that I can be other to myself *and* find that same otherness in the other *who is not me*, is forced to posit new violences that will try to mediate between the triad of man, God and state. The result, as we have seen, is to fail to do justice to the determination of infinity within social totality. I am already other and the other is not me – this is self-otherness, and self-otherness known as the other who is not me. This is the *Aufhebung*, the recollection of truth learning about its own misrecognition. It is the openness of the negation of the negation because it is the truth of learning that it remains open to its own misrecognition rather than overcoming it or closing it down. Alterity in Hegel is a double negative, but only a single education.

Error as actual vulnerability

The same point can now be made slightly differently in regard to education in Hegel as the actuality of error. Actuality is one of Hegel's most important educational concepts. It is well known, for example, that in the *Preface* to the *Philosophy of Right* he stated that 'what is rational is actual and what is actual is rational' (1967: 10). The conservative tone of this comment is seemingly backed up by others in the *Preface*, notably that philosophy always comes about too late to instruct the world on how it ought to be and that the owl of Minerva flies only at dusk, at the end of the day. Philosophy appears here to be the science only of hindsight. Yet it is the significance of the philosophical education that hindsight carries as recollection that requires to be comprehended.

There are two points here. First, recollection is not restricted to looking backwards. This is because a present recollection is also open to itself as a future recollection. In other words, we can know that this present will be recollected in the future. We will be known again, and truthfully, when our truth is negated, re-formed and re-learned. Our mastery over the past is nonesuch because we do not have mastery over the present. This is the groundlessness of recollection in and for itself. Recollection backwards is

also recollection forwards.[11] As such, its actuality includes but does not prioritize its being known as yet to be known. This is not undecideability. It is
the knowing of the truth of undecideability.

Second, if the recollection of what was and the future recollection of what
is are seen as error in the sense that they are only knowledge for us, and not
knowledge in itself, then *all* knowing is error. But the judgement of this as
error presupposes that the object of thought stands on one side and the
thought of it on the other. In fact, Hegel's political education is based on
the insight that error is itself the universality of all thought, because all
thought is recollection.[12] If error contains universality then the truth of this
requires to be known. One way to proceed here would be Socratic, and to
say that this is the universality of ignorance, that we know only that we do
not and cannot know anything. But Socrates, too, holds the universality of
error still only as error. It is in the negation of the negation, and therefore
in education in Hegel, that the universality of ignorance is comprehended,
that is, that error itself is true. This, as we have been arguing, is the nature
of education in Hegel. In several of the chapters above we have seen how,
when the actuality of death in life – negation of negation – is eschewed, it
defines otherness *per se*. The idea that negation in thought is only error –
that error is 'other' than truth – is just such an exporting of death. If the
truth of error is comprehended, as it is in education in Hegel, then death
has become its own groundless absolute knowing, and, again, it is only
learning that can hold the truth of such negation as its own actuality. Levinas, in casting truth beyond the error of totality, is in fact avoiding the truth
of the vulnerability that is so central and yet at times so far from his work.

Educational imperative

Finally in this chapter to the question of education as a moral imperative.
Does education in Hegel feed the other with bread from its own mouth?
Levinas's political philosophy is so appealing because it appears to offer a
transcendental, perhaps categorical, perhaps unconditional imperative that
I am commanded by the Other to feed the stranger over and above my own
needs. Does anything in Hegel come close to this? It does. The question for
the master here is not, as in Levinas, am I commanded to give, for it is in the
nature of mastery that one master can refuse another. The question really
is how do I learn that the command is just? The answer is that one can only
experience the command within the social relations that already shape the
command and its reception, and that means experiencing the command,
the imperative, as an autoimmunity. To help the other is to oppose myself.
Accepted at face value, I can react to the command as being impossible or

unwelcome, and walk past the stranger who needs help; or I can help in bad conscience; or I can give food to the first stranger but not to the second. Each of these responses speaks from within the impossibility of the unconditional command. But philosophically, I can learn of the significance of the truth of this impossibility, that it is in the impossibility that I am able to learn why and how giving bread is my own truth in relation to myself as well as to the other. It is when I learn that the command to love thy neighbour as thyself is within the experience where I am already other and the other is not me, that it offers an education different from that found in Levinas. I am commanded to give only because I know the other to be other to my otherness.

Thus, it is not that we are the same that commands my generosity. It is that I can recognize the difference of the other in myself, even though I can never have this as an abstract mutual recognition. This is perhaps the most fundamental difference between Levinas and Hegel regarding the relation of self and other. The imperative in education in Hegel is not just to feed the stranger but to know why to feed him, which means to know the truth of our relationship and thus also to know the stranger in my own otherness. That I should treat my neighbour as myself carries the imperative of double negation where I am already other and the other is not me. How else could I know to feed him unless his otherness to me and my otherness to myself learn of themselves within the impossibility of their being the same?

Generosity, here, is autoimmune, and difficult, because as master I have to accept generosity as an antagonistic self-education. Giving reveals me as the face-to-face of life and death. As life I am already death in life, I am already other to myself. But death is not me and therefore I am not the other. Giving plays out this crisis of identity, and is an education that carries its own imperative. Learning generosity is hard because generosity is never enough, it is never a blank cheque. This aporia of giving educates us regarding self and other. When I give I have to suffer this education, namely that I am already other and yet the other is not me. I am not fulfilled in my giving and this lack of fulfilment is exactly the truth of giving, the truth of death in life. The imperative of education in Hegel is not simply to give or to be generous; it is to risk the learning that it offers us. To do justice to the other here is the imperative of education in Hegel. Or, of course, one could sell all one has and give it to the poor – but the man (and, indeed, the nation) were sorrowful on hearing this, for he was very rich.[13]

Notes

[1] Levinas's view that such a criticism is facile will be returned to below.

² In a chapter which in essence is arguing that Levinas's notion of the absolutely unassimilable Other is an oxymoron, the question of the capitalization of 'other' is raised. In upper case it is the ineffability of God that is prioritized, whereas in lower case it is absolute knowing that is veiled. That said, I retain capitalization for Levinas's absolutely Other as it keeps in view its opposition to otherness in Hegel. The ambiguity that the other – say, the stranger – is the Other in Levinas is retained, where appropriate, by the use of Other. I have not, however, amended any direct quotations.

³ Levinas uses the notion of recollection here (*se recueillir* and *le recueillement*) to describe the revelation of the transcendent in the welcome of the feminine face. See Levinas, 1969: 150–5; 1961: 124–8.

⁴ For a philosophy of the teacher working with education in negation, and with the truth of the teacher therein, see Tubbs (2005b).

⁵ In a private letter, Howard describes *Levinas and the Political* as 'a bleak read'.

⁶ There is not space to compare Levinas with Derrida here. We can note, however, that the totality of war is a similar effect to the totality of difference-opposition, and that its incompletion is its autoimmunity.

⁷ The full paragraph from Caygill here reads as follows: 'As part of the Diaspora he has, according to his own theory, not only the right but the obligation to question those actions of the State of Israel that are idolatrous or that diverge from its prophetic inspiration. Indeed we shall see that, on some occasions, Levinas did act according to his political principles, but also that on others he remained silent or, it might be argued, privileged the work of the state over the prophetic principles of the work of justice. The possibility of the latter – in the face of Levinas's own thought – is not unconnected with the persistent discourse of sacrifice that attends his reflections on Israel. This cannot but bring him into an uncomfortable proximity with idolatry and the risk of the consequent deflation of his own political and ethical thought' (2002: 176).

⁸ While Caygill concerns himself with the effect of this opposition on the political in Levinas, in fact it is an opposition that disrupts the whole of Levinas's project in *Otherwise than Being*. Significant here, as Caygill points out, is that Levinas abandons 'the language of metaphysics' (2002: 124) employed in *Totality and Infinity* in order to frame a 'project of religious and social theory' (2002: 124). The third party of metaphysics and politics, and of ego and alterity in *Totality and Infinity*, becomes divided from itself in *Otherwise than Being* and portrayed as two middles, as illeity and justice.

⁹ The arguments presented now until the end of the chapter lean heavily on what has been presented above in Chapters 1 and 2.

¹⁰ We have been carrying this ambiguity as Other.

¹¹ Kierkegaard calls this 'repetition' forwards, but I have kept recollection here to illustrate better its autoimmunity to itself; see Kierkegaard (1983). See also footnote 11 of *Introduction*.

¹² This is the same insight that Nietzsche noted in the historical man and is Zarathustra's most abysmal thought, that all 'I will' is really only 'what was'. *Ressentiment* here is the will's refusal to accept the universal nature of this 'error'.

¹³ Matt. 19.22; Lk. 18.23.

Chapter 6

I-Philosophy

[N]o wise man ever wished to be younger.

(*Swift, 1886: 113*)

[I]t can be said that man is prior to the boy in substance and completion, but the boy is before the man in generation and in time.

(*Aquinas, 1998: 25*)[1]

Introduction

This chapter reconstructs the *Phenomenology of Spirit* as a spiritual education of the *modern reflective subject*. It does so in order to illustrate the spiritual education that is carried in and by the Western experience of self and other. It retrieves, or recollects, the stages of spirit's phenomenological education as stages in the spiritual life of a modern reflective subject from childhood, youth and adulthood to old age.

The *Phenomenology* is the story of the spiritual education of the West from Ancient Greece to early nineteenth century Europe.[2] Its dynamic is the way that life, in its perspective as victor over death, continually misrecognizes itself as independent from its struggle with death. The forms that this misrecognition takes are self and other, both within the one individual – the I – and external to him – the We. Death continually returns in the form of negation to teach life, or the self, of the truth it is suppressing. These negations are the shapes taken by spiritual education, and the *Aufhebung* they carry is actual in the recollection of itself as spirit.

As we will see, this spiritual education comes to know itself in and as the recollection that is life in death and death in life, or as absolute spirit. But, equally important, this *philosophical* education is still the truth of the individual reflective subject who is already other to himself and to the (external) other. The *Aufhebung* of these two negations has its subject and substance in preserving the negations in philosophical education, and not in any final overcoming of the reflective subject who is being educated in this way.

This education is actual, then, in and as *I-philosophy*, that is, as the individual who learns himself. I-philosophy is recollection as absolute spirit and is the learning that knows itself as the science of experience. It is as I-philosophy that Hegel's philosophies of Right, Religion, etc. are written. However, in this chapter we will restrict ourselves to the spiritual education formative of I-philosophy in the *Phenomenology*.

Both the content and the structure of the *Phenomenology* are part of this education. As such, it is a spiritual education unlike that, for example, of Augustine in *The Confessions* or al-Ghazali in *Deliverance from Error*. While it involves spirit's confession to itself regarding its own mistakes in its experiences of thinking the true, this confession takes a modern form in the diremption of the I and the We. Included among these mistakes is the idea that this spiritual education is simply chronological, as for example the education outlined by Rousseau in *Emile*. In fact, spiritual education in Hegel works backwards as recollection as much as it works forwards as development. It is part of the method of the *Phenomenology* to disrupt chronology in line with the ambiguities of the education it is following, while at the same time still being a discernible development.

Hegel described the *Phenomenology* as a science of the experience of consciousness. This means that the structure of the book is determined by how thought works rather than how history appears. In the *Phenomenology* thought is concerned to find *its* history in chronological history. This development works behind the back of chronological history as spiritual education. When this latter can recollect its own development, spiritual education has determined itself as absolute spirit. But this is not *just* another dogmatic historical standpoint. It is *also* that which knows itself in its own groundlessness, its absolute negation, in and as its learning of this groundlessness. As we have seen in previous chapters, only learning can be the something of the nothing. This is the truth of old age, as we will come to see, and it is the eternal circle *and* finite education that constitutes absolute spirit and that is known in and as education in Hegel. Therefore, the stages in spiritual education of childhood, youth, adulthood and old age that we will follow are not simply the chronological development of the reflective subject. They are, rather, the component parts of the recollection that knows them as itself. Spiritual personal development and chronological personal development may coincide to varying extents, but the former refer to a spiritual education that a subject may or may not have during his life. Indeed, such a spiritual education may be precisely what is missing in the contradictions and aporias lived out within the chronology of a reflective subject's life.

Nor are the stages of childhood, youth, etc. arbitrarily applied to spiritual development. They arise within the recollection of spirit when it looks back at the different characteristics of its own development. Also, because education in the *Phenomenology* and in this chapter is one of recollection, this education begins not with the child but with the modern reflective subject in the social world who recalls his becoming this recollection. Childhood is its immediacy; youth is its time of uncertainty in mediation; adulthood is the certainty of the self; and old age is the whole that recollects these stages as itself, as I-philosophy. There is no certainty however, that spirit's development will match the facts of any individual life. As Hegel is reported to have said when asked about the difference between philosophy and facts, *so much the worse for the facts.*

There is one final point to be made here before turning to the *Phenomenology* directly. The modern political subject is defined as free in his separation from, and not in his union with, the other. As such, modern political experience is dualistic, divided between the individual and the social. The social is other to the free individual, and his experience of law and of its categorical imperatives is, at worst, one of heteronomy and, at best, one of aporia. This determines how the modern person sees his own development, that is, as a relation to himself and, separately, as a relation to others. In what follows I have found it helpful to call the latter a sociological education. Sociology articulates these tensions between self and society in many forms. But a sociology of sociology is needed if this experience of contingency, where the I is torn between personal and social freedoms that contradict each other, is to be able to comprehend itself as a shape of philosophical and spiritual education. That the *Phenomenology* is structured in this way is in itself a recognition of its own moments within and contingent upon essentially modern social and political relations.

It will be helpful at this point to say a little about the way the chapter is now organized. It has two main divisions. Part A recollects the education of the I, and Part B recollects this education as the I that is We. It is common in work on Hegel to call these the stages of reason and spirit, respectively, but I want these terms to emerge in the education and I have therefore given priority to the terms I and We. In each of the Parts A and B there is the development from childhood to youth to adulthood. The repetition of the headings is also the return of the I and the We to each other. The chapter ends with a section on absolute knowing as old age which recollects the whole of itself in life and death, or more accurately as death in life.

We begin then in the recollection of the immediate beginning of the reflective subject, that is, in childhood.

PART A

Childhood

Childhood for Hegel is the time of immediacy, that is, of a consciousness that consists of will without responsibility to itself. Consciousness begins with the awareness of objects through the senses, objects that, as such, are immediately present. The child learns most in these early years because he is open to the outer world and all that it introduces to his senses. But this sense-certainty will be unable to sustain itself in such immediacy, for objects come and go. How is the child to know these objects when they are not present to his senses? This is the same as asking how the child can deal with the change from 'this is' to 'it was'. The absence forces a change in consciousness, where the object is now the thought of the object. This thought is, as it were, the result of the loss of immediacy, even though at this early stage it may only be an immediate thought. The child will also attempt to give himself a presence in the world. Immediate at first, this too will suffer the failure of immediacy, where this presence is opposed by other such presences. Put together, these two experiences of the loss of immediacy force the child into a different stance in the world, one which is gradually developing into the impermanence of all objects, that is, into their being thought. Thought, then, gradually becomes aware of itself as the 'I' or the ego of the child. The I, here, is the instability of immediacy becoming known to it and is experienced as will.

This will has to learn of itself as part of the failure of immediacy. Objects are perceived as stable only in the knowing of them, and they are known only in contact to other objects. Perception differentiates objects according to their properties and conceptualizes them, even if only in memory to begin with. But this is the beginning of understanding in the child, for it is where the world is known according to its being thought. This understanding of the world is itself immediate. Hegel argues here for the child's early education beyond the family to be one that does not prioritize the immediacy of the world in feeling and in the senses over the failure of such immediacy to sustain itself and the thoughts of the world that this induces. The child needs to think the world, for this is how and where the path to adulthood and to freedom begins. To fetishize the feeling at this stage in the child's education risks encouraging a merely arbitrary response to the world of objects and other people.

Hegel's comments here will not please those progressive educators who see play as the most important method of a child discovering the world and the rules that govern interaction with others. Hegel favours discipline over play. Play has its place in the child's life but it is not to be seen as the way in which the child will best learn of social life. Hegel's fear is that learning of mediation through play will deny the child the seriousness of mediation, an experience which is absolutely necessary for a formative education in the demands of freedom. Perhaps Hegel's concerns here are particularly sharp when seen against the present form and content of the culture industry in the West that sells entertainment and fun in life as more desirable, more worthwhile, even more meaningful than the seriousness of thought that freedom and its effects on others demands. Freedom to have mass produced fun is freedom separated from its own dialectic of command and obedience, or mastery and service. Relevant here, then, is Hegel's comment that the child 'must obey in order that he may learn to command. Obedience is the beginning of all wisdom' (1990: 60, *zusatz*), adding that 'the most rational thing that children can do with their toys is to break them' (1990: 59, *zusatz*). This obedience, however, need not be seen as cruel or dictatorial and Hegel is clear in his own pedagogy that the learning of obedience is necessary for the truth of a man's independence in the world. The truth of independence is in obedience, not to others, but to the self that must live with others. It is also the case that examples of education in obedience given by Hegel are learning the alphabet and learning of order in the natural world. Here obedience to structure is also an experience in abstracting from sense-certainty and is therefore also a development of the understanding, for, again, it is part of the forces that constitute perception of objects in thought.

However, the understanding here that is based on perception will have to face its own limited scope and, ultimately, its failure to hold to its immediacy. A child may understand what a leaf is and what a bird is, but this understanding only raises another set of issues. These concern the relation of one's thought to the world that it knows. In its most insistent form this is the question repeated by the child as to 'why' things in the world are as they are. Here is the experience that thought can be more powerful than the world it knows, for it can demand answers to questions raised but not answered by the world. The understanding is insufficient to satisfy itself on the appearance of the world in thought. The understanding, as it were, reports on objects in the world but such reporting only raises further and deeper questions. It is in this instability of the understanding that the understanding comes to understand itself. This is where the consciousness of the child becomes the self-consciousness of youth.

Youth

No preacher is listened to but Time, which gives us the same train and turn of thought that older people have tried in vain to put into our heads before.

(*Swift, 1886: 109*)

Youth takes its beginning in the certainty of its own self-consciousness. It does not need to remember that it has arisen from the frailty of the understanding for it takes itself to be the beginning of all knowledge. Youth knows best. This certainty, however, is grounded in the separation of thought from the real world. Spiritual education here sees self-consciousness looking only to itself for truth. Its freedom consists in the fact that, as self-consciousness, it is not mastered by any other or any thing. Here youth enjoys an indifference to the world, but it is an indifference that can take different forms. Youth appears self-centred, self-obsessed and thinks the world revolves around it.[3] However, one form of this self-centredness is an idealism about how the world is and how it should be, although it shows little or no benefit of actually having had any contact or experience with the 'real world'. Thought here is in search of its own purity and integrity within self-consciousness, a purity that is tied to its separation from the real world and one that is true only to the thought of the world.

Accompanying this idealism self-consciousness can take the shape of a disbelief in all claims to truth in and by the real world. Certainty becomes something certain only of the untruths of the world. All truths that are asserted over and against this scepticism collapse in the wake of their competing with each other; opposed to every account there is another equal account. This scepticism can be nihilistic and destructive in its indifference. Youth can be the rebel who serves self-certainty in the negation of the world, and does so, at first, by holding this negativity to be the ground of his certainty. But the cost of the standpoint of this rebel is that his certainty in the lack of truth cannot survive its own negation, its own undermining. The (negative) spiritual lesson here is that the indifference of self-consciousness to the world cannot ground itself in order to preserve this indifference. Self-consciousness becomes indifferent to itself and suffers the same negative fate as it held for the real world. This is the beginning of a very unhappy spiritual education for youth, one in which the certainty of self-consciousness opposes itself. Its own certainty turns against itself and leaves self-consciousness and its truth rent asunder. This self-consciousness is now dualistic and inwardly torn apart. It is essentially self-contradictory, and is other to itself in the way that previously the external was other to it. This stage of spiritual education is not just the loss of truth but also the impossibility of ever knowing truth. Thought contradicts every truth it comes across. It is a very destructive experience for youth in that it can find no rest from its doubts about the world and about itself. It despairs in a sense of hopelessness that knows no possible reconciliation between thought and truth.

The youth here is open to many different influences that claim a meaning that can restore self-consciousness from its negativity to a positivity. One response to this unhappiness is a faith in the eternal and the beyond, whilst another is attachment to an ideal of a society yet to be achieved. Both in a sense are idealistic. But experiments with such solutions inevitably repeat the same contradictions, and youth is plunged further into despair with each repetition. Youth's search for meaning in life expresses the pain born of deep and fundamental unhappiness at the relation between truth and the I for whom it appears.

However, this unhappiness in fact already contains the seeds of the *Aufhebung* that will retrieve and recollect meaning from within the despair. The independent self-consciousness that negates the world and negates itself now shares its negativity with the world. This can be a cruel education for at its heart is the recognition of the complicity of idealism and rebellion with the world they oppose. Youth comes to see that it did no more than repeat the very uncertainties in itself that it accused the world of. The solution, as it were, always becomes part of the problem. This return of the negative to the self-consciousness that exported it to the external world is the education that now brings youth and the world together. Out of the experience that thought and the world cannot be separated comes a new reality for self-consciousness. This new reality sublates the unhappiness of youth and his negation of self and world. This realizes a standpoint wherein thought sees that in and through its negative self and work it has exercised a totality, in that what it has done it has done to itself. This is no longer freedom from the world. Now this is the freedom of thought as comprehensively self-determining of itself and the world. The self-consciousness that recollects itself in this new freedom is the thought that thinks the truth of all reality, and this is *reason*. Now the youth enters adulthood because reason becomes him. More colloquially, this is where idealism realizes the truth and necessity of 'selling out' to the adult world as it is. However, as we will see now, the recollection of the development and negativity of self-consciousness that formed the rational and comprehensive idea of itself is forgotten when reason takes itself abstractly as being the consciousness of truth and being the truth as consciousness, that is, as adult.

Emile and Sophie

If we look for a moment to Rousseau's *Emile*, we find that this ambivalence is not found in the education that Rousseau provides for his pupil. As his tutor in fact he ensures that Emile does not experience the unhappiness of the I either in relation to its own negation or the negation of the social world. Indeed, Emile is kept free from any tension between the development of his own needs and the demands of his civil society, the demand, that is, for *amour-propre*, for conformity to social – and for Rousseau, hypocritical and unjust – norms and values. Emile is educated beyond the city and as such moves from childhood to adult via a period of youth that is not self-contradictory, not as it were, torn between the freedom of the I and social conformity. Emile's youth is spent learning about freedom in physical but not in actual political relations. He moves from play to work without an intervening education into the freedom of his own self-consciousness and its negations and returns. In other words, Emile is denied the formative political education of life in the aporia of the free-thinking I in the unfree world.

One might see this as a successful education in that the excesses of bourgeois individualism have been avoided, with the result that Emile knows only true needs and thus only forms social relationships grounded in integrity. However, the real cost of this smooth transition from boy to man is borne by Sophie. On her befall the contradictions that Emile is protected from. She has to know intricately the workings of bourgeois civil society if she is to survive in the social world. Hers is a full political education into the self-interest and power of male bourgeois individualism and into the need, therefore, for her to formulate a political response. This response is to learn how to play the game in ways that ensure she has some political control over her life and its events. Yet her lack of freedom is for all that a more significant political education than Emile receives. Her education is where fashion and freedom oppose one another to the extent that freedom is re-formed and re-conceptualized according to the political actualities that face Sophie. However, this education is refused a rationality beyond that of necessary artifice. Sophie has no opportunity for the *Aufhebung* in which her dilemma can become transformative recollection because she must remain wedded to the life that alienates freedom from political reason. She must remain free only in the sense that she must find new ways to display her power of attraction over her man, a power which, as Rousseau makes clear, is absolutely grounded in her powerlessness.

Thus, while Emile has reason without the experience of political actuality, Sophie has the experience of political unfreedom without reason. Yet perhaps remarkably, there is an *Aufhebung* in *Emile*. Rousseau points out that it is in the unity of these differences between Emile and Sophie that power and powerlessness are both developed and re-formed. The power of Emile discovers its dependence upon Sophie, and in turn the powerlessness of Sophie recognizes the power that it holds over Emile. There is also recollection in *Emile*, for Rousseau has his student come to thank him for the formative experiences he has engineered for him, seeing in hindsight how necessary they were. However, Emile has not been educated for the world as it is and will not comprehend freedom except in his relation to Sophie, but even here the freedom of the master is the freedom that has exported its own truth in vulnerability to the other, to Sophie. The return of this vulnerability, and the formal equality of Emile and Sophie remained beyond Rousseau's time.

Adulthood

The adult enjoys the certainty of himself as at one with the realities of the social world. He is reason that is in and for itself, for there is no contradiction between his own idea of himself and the idea that the world has of him. His thought of reality and his own lived reality are no longer at odds with each other. This is where the doubts and uncertainties of youth are sublated into the positive unity of the I and his world. This world is his world and, having negated the illusory freedom he had as a youth, where the real world was merely a beyond, it now reinforces the freedom of the sovereign rational person who is one among other such sovereign rational persons. Thus, the education of youth to adulthood becomes fixed as the rite of passage into the reality of the social world, a reality in which the I knows its responsibilities for work, family and community.

However, the adult seldom remembers the path that has led to this new certainty, and therefore this I appears as a natural standpoint. It forgets that the truth of reason lies in the experiences that have formed it. This is never more obvious than in the relation between adult and youth. The adult forgets his own youth when educating his children, and is particularly agitated with the 'attitude' of youth. It is also the case that youth cannot understand the adult for the former has not travelled the path that determines the adult. Thus the adult forgets that the child moves from sense-certainty to ego-certainty, and that with the latter there is a freedom from the world that allows comment and criticism upon it without the binds of commitment to it.

There seems to be here an implicit conservatism in adulthood, particularly in the demand for the youth to become adult and to accept his responsibilities. This returns the I from its idealistic freedom to its complicity within the world it rejects. Yet Hegel does not see this conformism as suppressing entirely the possibility of new meaning in the world. In the adulthood of civil society there remains scope for 'honourable, far reaching and creative activity [for this is not] a dead, absolutely inert world but, like the life-process, a world which perpetually creates itself anew, which while merely preserving itself, at the same time progresses' (1990: 62–63, *zusatz*). This is the nature of the *Aufhebung* in Hegelian philosophical education. It is where change is arbitrary, even terroristic, unless it is able to preserve what it negates in a new, developed and negated form.

This, indeed, is the integrity of the *Aufhebung*, that it neither wholly discards its previous shapes nor imports into itself anything from outside that will suppress the immanent power to educate and develop. Thus, the nature of 'change' that the spiritual education of the adult brings about is an education, also, about what 'change' means. We might say here that spiritual education requires one always to understand the nature of change within development, culture and *Aufhebung* so that one's natural consciousness does not act blindly in the world against the actuality of change and often therein against the very people one intends to benefit. This integrity is the subjective substance of the education of youth into adulthood. Thus, Hegel says, 'on the one hand we can say that the man only creates what is already there; yet on the other hand, his activity must also bring about an advance' (1990: 63, *zusatz*). This ambivalence is the protection against terror and has that protection as part of the change it brings about. The integrity is the ambivalence, and it is what makes youth despair of the seeming indifference of the adult world to real social change.

As reason, then, the adult can only see youth as yet to understand the totality or the real world, and is impatient at the arrogance of the self-consciousness that knows so much only because it knows so little. But the certainty of the adult now fares little better, and will undergo its own experiences of failures, negations and transitions. Having forgotten the path to adulthood, the adult is reason only immediately as far as the child and the youth are concerned, and they experience this adult as thinking himself right without having to justify this. This is reason without reason, and is the immediate appearance of the authority of the adult, an empirical but not (yet) a spiritual authority. But immediate reason cannot withstand the relation to itself that thought brings about here. It cannot remain unchanged by the demand that it justify itself universally, for this means that the universality of the adult must become an object for him, and therefore separated from him. The adult is called upon to think its own universality, a contradiction that defeats itself. Just as in the life and death struggle life made its negation other to it, so the adult here makes his negation other to him. This is the same negation that realized itself as reason out of its own unhappiness regarding its relation to the true. Thus it makes external the experience that it depends upon. It externalizes its own truth. As such, this truth appears as an object over and against it as universal law. Law here is to reason and the adult what death is to life. Both the adult and life have to find themselves again in that which they have eschewed. Law, a universality, is other to the adult whose truth it is. As such, this other is *all* rational self-conscious adults. The truth of the adult therefore is other people. This is reason as social relation, or ethical life, or again, as society. Only when the adult learns that he is this same relation to himself as he is to other people will his spiritual education be recollected by spirit as its own development. It is this spiritual education of the adult in relation to society that we will now follow.

Of course, this is not the first time that self-consciousness has become aware of ethical or social life. Indeed, as we will see in a moment, ethical life has been present throughout its education. The point is, however, that they are separated in our account of this education because that is the structure of our modern experience of spirit, that is, that the I is claimed and opposed by the political totality in which it finds itself. It is this experience, now, that will begin a new education for the adult. His relation to others has always been formative for him, but now he must recollect the ways in which this has been so. What lies ahead for this reflective person is an education about how universality as other has also grown and developed spiritually. In a sense the education of the adult must begin again, in the childhood and youth of spirit. The adult, who judges the youth, must now judge himself in the same terms, that is, about how much he knows because of how little he knows. Thus this education begins negatively with the loss of the certainty of the rational person to the totality of ethical or social life.

PART B

I As We

Spiritual education, like that of personal education, takes its beginning
from the reflective mind of the adult. This adult now seeks to understand
how his dependency upon others – the We – compromises his individual
sovereignty. In essence this is a sociological education. There are two truths
in this sentence. His education is sociological because it is dualistic. He is
trying to comprehend how society or social forms relate to the I as its truth.
This means that the reflective I is still posited as that from which the enquiry
into society can begin, as it was in beginning its enquiry into itself. Dualism
is built in to the very structure of such a sociological enquiry, but whilst
dualism carries out the enquiry, it leaves its own presupposition of itself out
of the enquiry. In other words, the essence of sociological enquiry is illusory. This is the second truth in the sentence that in essence this is a
sociological education. There is, therefore, a third partner in this sociology.
There is the consciousness that knows sociology to be compromised by its
own standpoint. *This* education teaches that the standpoint of the reflective
I and of his object of study is not just a study of the contingency of the former upon the latter. It is also a study carried out by contingency in the form
of the dualism of self and society. The shapes that this latter contingency
takes, the shapes of illusion, are the shapes of spirit now in the *Phenomenology*. They are present only in the ways in which they are posited. This third
partner is veiled and hard to see, but it remains the meaning and the significance, the actuality, of dualism. It is this triadic relation that is intended by
the dualism of I-philosophy. The third partner is present in appearing to be
absent. It takes the wisdom of old age to come to know this third partner as
the truth of its other 'truthful' appearances.

   We will begin now to look at spirit's education regarding its own development. We will follow this education through the same phases of childhood
and youth, although this time in the way they express themselves as social
or collective forms rather than in individual consciousness, self-consciousness and reason. Nevertheless we are still following this education in the
way it appears in and to the modern reflective subject. It is this subject that
has the following spiritual experiences, and it is only as a result of this education that we will be able to refer this sociological education as really a
spiritual education, for although they are all shapes of spirit, this only
appears in the spirit's recollection of itself in its old age. Equally we will see
the same structure of immediacy, mediation and *Aufhebung* moving this

education forwards at all levels such that particular developments take on a greater significance only when they become what is recollected.

Childhood

Spirit's immediacy is, like the consciousness of the child, only knowable to itself in a recollection that knows it to be lost. In the *Phenomenology* this immediacy is already the collapse of consciousness as the divine law and custom of Hellenic city-states, where spirit as the child is the tradition that binds together all its members in a common substance.

For our reflective subject these 'natural' social relationships begin in the immediate relations of the individual and ethical life, that is, as love in the family and as law in custom and tradition. When these immediacies hold the individual at one with the collective through feeling and emotion, and see such allegiance as virtue, then the nation becomes a family and shared blood becomes the tie of the social bond. But the consciousness of the people, if it is to ground its sovereignty objectively, must be thought of as something permanent and sustainable in the world beyond its immediate perception and understanding of itself. This process becomes even more urgent as the immediacy of the collective bond comes into contact with other such bonds in the world. This life and death struggle of immediacies is already the end of immediate 'natural' social life and is the beginning of political life. The mind that survives the struggle exports the death of itself as other than itself, which helps in turn to define *this* community against *that* community. But it is already too late for immediate ethical life here, for the child comes to see that it, the social collective, cannot sustain itself in feelings and emotions against this will becoming self-conscious. All ethical immediacies are in this sense the spirit of the child, a spirit which carries the fundamental ambivalence of immediate belonging and life in relation to otherness. Even though the other to the collective can be used to strengthen the intensity of the immediate bond, nevertheless in the other of ethical immediacy – and other here means both the other to immediacy and the otherness of immediacy to itself – the seeds of the collapse of immediate ethical life are already present. The natural ethical life cannot hold out against its division into otherness, a division that at first is concrete as the I of its citizens and as the law that recognizes them.

Youth

Youthful spirit takes its beginning in the certainty of the law that guarantees the rights of the person. This law is property law because the sovereignty of the person is based on the exclusion from him of the vulnerability that would compromise his legal identity. This is passed to non-persons, that is, to objects and to men deemed no better than objects. This certainty, however, cannot be at peace with itself. The law is a form of universality that, in eschewing vulnerability as other, denies to itself the means by which its vulnerability might come to know itself. Spirit, here, is an alienation of itself from itself. Divine law is the truth of the vulnerability alienated from itself and become absolutely other to the truth of the legal person. This person thus enters a period of most unhappy education in which political truth cannot be reconciled with divine truth, and where all attempts at trying to do God's work on earth merely emphasizes and repeats their separation. This is experienced as dualism but is accompanied by the third partner who is present not as the two sides of the separation, but as the relation they continually misrecognize. As dualism the truth of the antithesis of divine and temporal authority is cast beyond man, who is deemed to be the one at fault here, to the perfection of a being beyond man. Here, the alienation of freedom from itself finds truth in the only place it can, in a beyond that transcends all human imperfection. The result is a world in which truth is absent from real life and demands that it be established there. But all attempts to do so remain unaware of the third partner in the relationship. Hence they can only repeat, but not re-form, the pre-existing relation between God and man. The result is that all attempts to establish God's will and law on earth collapse in on themselves because they are only *human* attempts. Faith in the work goes hand-in-hand with lawlessness on earth and the result is barbarism. The harder faith struggles to bring God to earth, the greater the barbarity.

Youthful spirit mirrors here the unhappy youth of self-consciousness. The latter existed in the rupture between inner freedom and outer authority. Now, the legal person is caught between an idea of truth that is beyond him, and beyond everyone else, and a life where it becomes impossible to act for the good. It is not necessary that this person believes in God (though he may do) for that is not the philosophical significance of this form of ethical life. The significance here is *Bildung,* that is, the education of the reflective adult about the third partner than can express for him the contradictions in his life. His good actions turn out bad results, his noble actions turn out ignoble, his attempts to act beyond self-interest turn against themselves, each reinforcing the feeling that it is impossible to act in the world according to a good that seems to be possible only in the world beyond human weakness. He may retain faith in the idea of the good, or he may despair completely of the good and see intrigue as a fair response to a hopeless situation abandoned by God.

It is the third partner, however, that is to prove more powerful than either of these responses. Spirit is present here as the appearance of an alienation of itself, that is, as a diremption between God and man. This appearance is known precisely in the contradictions that plague the person. His failed attempts to reform the world re-form him in and as the culture of spirit.

It is here that the reflective adult who is sceptical regarding the possibility of any common bond between his self-interest and the community will learn that this is precisely what he *does* have in common with everyone else. His education here is that the good act is always compromised in being enacted. Self-interest is inescapable. This self-interest and the hypocrisy of the selfless act are the new spiritual universality. It is how this person now realizes that he is in fact part of objective social life. His complicity is his new education and it is an education, again, in the hypocrisy of the stance that holds itself separate from social life. The good act cannot hide from the hypocrisy of its self-interest, but equally, self-interest cannot hide from its need for social life. This is a new shape of spirit. On the one hand, it commits to reason the superstitions that have been employed by faith in bringing God's law to earth. On the other hand, it also commits to reason the hypocrisies of earthly authorities in masking self-interest behind spiritual benevolence. Youthful spirit now finds equality and universality out of its own self-oppositions. This shape of spirit is the enlightenment of spirit that it is the work of true universality when it opposes pseudo-universality. The person now knows the third partner in ethical life has all along been spirit in which the I and the We are always related, even at those times when that relation is obscured behind the intrigue of seemingly benevolent self-interest. He knows now that wars of self-interest are barbarism but he knows also that there exists a powerful force by which to oppose this self-interest, and this is the idea of the equality of all men. This, then, is the culture of spirit, the philosophical education that finds spirit in the truth of liberty, fraternity and equality.

Adulthood

If a man would register all his opinions upon love, politics, religion, learning etc., beginning from his youth and so go on to old age, what a bundle of inconsistencies and contradictions would appear at last.

(*Swift, 1886: 112*)

Spirit now embarks on the stage of its education where its abstract unity –
enlightenment – becomes an object to itself as morality. Here again our
reflective subject will experience spiritual education as one where an internal certainty becomes other to itself. This is the education of spirit into
adulthood.

   To begin with, the fervour and excitement of spirit finding itself to be the
equality of all men makes it forget the negations that constituted its self-
(re-)formation. Any new beginning means, again, that the third partner has
become another form of natural consciousness. Enlightenment here is the
immediacy of the equality of all men and is therefore only abstract. Its certainty justifies collective terror over and against individuals who set
themselves above this equality. But, in the demand for a justification of this
terror, the immediacy of spirit's certainty must become object to itself and,
again, other to itself. Its certainty therefore opposes itself in being known,
for in being known the strength of reason as equal in all men is also the
weakness of reason that it is in no man in particular and therefore in no
man at all save those who assert it as their own. Whether he chooses as his
cause equality within existing social relations or equality in revolutionized
social relations, the third partner will be suppressed if formal equality is
dominant over inwardness. This shape of ethical life is characterized as terror not just by the state but also in those modern political revolutions where
the term revolution best describes not the change that takes place but the
reproduction of the suppression of spirit, of the third partner, in such
upheaval.

   It is in this struggle of the inner and the outer of the person that spirit
becomes morality. The heterogeneity of the totality of abstract equality in
formal law is now opposed to the knower whose equality it is supposed to
embrace. This means that it is experienced internally as a further separation of the rational person and his collective truth. This internal experience
of formal universality is the education of spirit to morality, that is, to the
question of whether a man should find his spiritual certainty in the duties
that are commanded of him externally, or whether he should obey the duty
that comes to him against this externality, that is, the duty of his own conscience. His spiritual education here is this dilemma of subjectivity opposed
by substance. It has substance, however, as this dilemma, and this is what the
moral individual's spiritual education now consists in.

   The adult moral person might respond to this struggle by giving priority
in the moral experience to his conscience, and to his well-intentioned
actions in the world. Moral actions here are grounded in the certainty of
truth in the I. Here moral spirit becomes only internal and undifferentiated

from the I. The moral adult believes that he has grasped here the truth of his spiritual education, that truth in the world rests with the good intentions and the piety of the conscientious I. The only community he belongs to is the religious community that expresses the internal ground of conscience externally. His duty to conscience overrides his duty to the state and its laws.

But conscience already contains within it the seeds of its own higher education. It is grounded in a contradiction that it cannot survive. When conscience acts universally in the world, the world accepts it as only a particular or an individual conviction. Its claims to universality are only a matter of words, contradicted by its deeds. It does what *it* believes to be right. It is precisely because individual conscience lacks substance that any substance will do. This is both the ground of moral judgements and therefore also their lack of ground. Spiritual education here has its revel and repose in this aporia. The moral individual pays lip service to the universal but acts only as he wishes. This education has its subject and substance in the hypocrisy of his moral judgements. This is because the judge must judge himself and expose the opposition of universal and particular within him. Judgement here acts as the valet to the moral hero, knowing the details of the life behind the grand appearance. When our moral adult judges himself he has his moral actions as other to himself. In this he might expect a form of mutual recognition for in confessing his hypocrisy he is other to himself and therefore other *qua* other. But as we have seen, this is not the structure of spiritual education regarding self and other. The other to the confessor is a hard-hearted judge who does not believe the veracity of the confessor. Even in this negation of the I by itself, the other is not this I. This lack of mutual recognition can see the moral adult return from his outer confession into an inner certainty of the beautiful soul which refuses further risk of non-mutual recognition. Lacking recognition it pursues an ascetic pining for that which the world cannot provide.

However, a lack of mutual recognition is already a spiritual education regarding self and other, as we have seen elsewhere in this book. The spiritual education of the moral subject consists in his double loss or negation. He loses to the We the truth he found in conscience, *and* he loses the truth of *this* loss when seeking its mutual recognition in others. Here the I is already other and the other is not the I. This is the self-determinate shape of spirit in its moral development. The *Aufhebung* of its development and self-opposition now teaches spirit something new about itself. It cannot achieve the unification of the moral adult with all other such adults but these two losses can recollect themselves as how the I and the We are negatively related.

It has passed through various stages of this non-achievement, from its immediate childhood, to its youthful culture and its sense of adult responsibility.
Now in its *Aufhebung* it has the recollection of this development and negation as the story of its own becoming. It *is* this education.

What is spirit to make of this? It comes to see that it is the dualism of subject and substance known in and as the relation that separates them. The
relation can only be known in retrospect, as its own recollection of itself.
Spirit here is educated to know itself as this education, for here it has
learned that what is lost is also retained in and as that learning.

Summary

Before looking at this learning in and for itself, it might be helpful to offer
a summary of the spiritual education of the reflective subject that we have
just described. The spiritual I begins as an ego and a will in the world which
then, in its self-consciousness, has itself as its own object. This I, however,
suffers from this separation in itself. It has doubt attached to everything it
thinks, believing thought to be unable to hold truth in itself. Certainty
therefore becomes something of a lost cause, something that can only lie in
an idealism beyond the real world. This I is characterized by its unhappiness in this separation, an unhappiness that can take a variety of forms
ranging from utter scepticism to a faith in the idea of the beyond, be it God
or an alternative form of society. The way out of this unhappiness is for the
I to join the real world and to receive the certainties that it can offer. The
I is now an adult but he can be as far away from knowing his spiritual education here as it is possible to be, for the rewards of joining society can seduce
the I away from his spiritual dilemmas.

The spiritual education of this I continues, however, when he experiences
the vulnerability of such certainties. These vulnerabilities arise in his work
in the social world with others like himself, when he realizes that his certainties are not justified against the certainties of others. This is the
beginning of his sociological education regarding his contingency upon
social relations.

At first the I experiences the social bond as something missing and knows
this lack because his own certainties are not universal in an immediate ethical unity with others. This lack is again an unhappiness for him because the
bond that he seeks seems torn between the irreconcilability of uncertain
social relations and true relations posited beyond his earthly existence. It
seems to him that there can be no paradise on earth, and that in fact his
social life is paradise lost. But his social bond is retrieved in knowing that all
rational men are equal with one another and deserve equal recognition

and respect. However, he finds that this principle is easier in theory than in practice. His own actions in the world seem always to repeat a conflict between self-interest and universal brotherhood. In the final part of his social education he realizes that because he is rational and accountable for his own actions, he must look inwardly for the justification of his actions and not seek external justification. This is the social man for whom social responsibility rests in his own conscience. But even here there is trouble, because from the point of view of everyone else one man's conscience can justify anything. His attempts to ground a true social relation end only in an arbitrariness of action and a hypocrisy of justification.

Only here is spirit able to understand itself as having been the substance in these subjective experiences. There are two losses here: the loss of the I to the social and loss of the social to the I. These losses have their truth in the recollection or the learning that results from them. The negations are not overcome, but they are productive of themselves as subject and substance in the education of the I that recollects them as its own self-(re-)formation. This is not mutual recognition, but it is the education in Hegel in which I am already other and the other is not me. This is the spiritual education in Hegel of the I that is We and the We that is I.

How is spirit now to represent this education as it looks back at the journey of self and society, this time in the awareness that it was present all the time? It can find itself present in the sensuous representations of religion and art, but I do not intend to pursue here this education in representation. Instead I turn now to spirit's relation to itself as education. This is the view realized in old age.

Old age

I am my own heir.
(Lope de Vega[4])

We shall not cease from exploration
And the end of all our exploring
Will be to arrive where we started
And know the place for the first time.

(T. S. Eliot, 1944: 43)

Old age here is not to be measured in years but in the wisdom of the actuality of recollection. The old man does not overcome the adult, nor does the adult overcome the child. The child is in the adult as the adult is in the old man.[5] This is the integrity of the *Aufhebung*. It preserves what it changes such that 'change' means the re-forming that pertains to education, to learning. Education is the only form that thinking takes in which it can retain what is changed in its being changed, for both are contained in the learning that knows change in this way. The old man is the philosophical adult; the adult is the philosophical child; the child is the philosophical old man; and all of them are spiritual shapes of the reflective subject whose spiritual education we have been following. The co-existence of these shapes in recollection is absolute spirit, and is I-philosophy. This, in a nutshell, is to know the comprehensive nature of spiritual education in Hegel.

Old age recollects how the relation of self and other is self-determinative as the spiritual education to I-philosophy. The *Phenomenology* has chronicled the individual and sociological enquiries into the relation of the reflective subject and his social world. In old age absolute spirit recollects that the different shapes of this relation always presupposed natural standpoints that hid behind various veils their own genesis in the experience of life and death and its actuality as the relation of self and other. On the one hand, the spiritual education of the reflective subject led to the recollection of his otherness to himself. On the other hand, he learned that his otherness could not easily be reconciled with the otherness of other such subjects. What absolute spirit has learned from both of these journeys is that the shapes of self and other were not only its own misrecognitions of itself, but were, at root, shapes of life and death. Now, in recollection, it finds its misrecognitions of life and death to be a totality in the *Aufhebung* of its development and negations. Absolute spirit, in recollection, knows that it is already other and that the other is not it. As such the old man is returned to life and death as the whole of I-philosophy for he knows now that his spiritual education has been formative in the myriad misrecognitions of life and death and in the loss of those misrecognitions to negation. Thus we end this chapter by looking briefly at how this absolute knowing of self and other as life and death is formative of philosophical wisdom in and of old age. The old man, facing his own death, recollects the truth of I-philosophy in this return to and of life and death.

Death only becomes actual in the life in which it is known. Its absence is its actuality and is how death exists in life. But it has also been a point of controversy throughout the history of Western philosophy as to what happens after death. Socrates did not fear death because he was open about his ignorance of it, and asked himself why would he be scared unless he presupposed that he knew something about what comes after death? The mediaevalists generally held the view that man, created by God who is eternal, must also have an eternal soul that will, after death, return to its creator. But education in Hegel turns this on its head. The wisdom of old age, here, is to know that eternity, too, is actual and can only be recollected from within the present. The prejudice that the subjective thinking of eternity is an error is grounded in the illusions of an unhappy spiritual education. The 'beyond' of the eternal is a finite prejudice grounded in the illusion of the reflective subject. The old man has seen such othering return many times in his spiritual journey and now recollects the truth in education of the eternal in the present. In his wisdom he sees recollection as the actuality of eternity and knows that the fear of error in knowing the absolute is really the error itself. Life *is* death. Life is the actuality of the eternity known as death. The life we lead has been an education towards knowing eternity in the finite.

This means for the old man that the thought of life *after* death takes on a different and recollective significance. We have seen that education in Hegel is death in life, but is there also life in death? What happens when death wins the life and death struggle? What is the view of the victor in that case? Religion and philosophy in the Western tradition have often argued for some form of resurrection of body and soul, or of the soul without the body. This is to say that when death is the victor over life, nevertheless life is still carried in and by death (as death has previously been carried in and by life). Some also see life after death as a metaphor for how the memory of the deceased lives on in friends, family, books and anything else that counts as a legacy. From Ecclesiastes comes the thought that 'I perceive that there is nothing better, than that a man shall rejoice in his own works; for that is his portion' (Ecc. 3.22) before he returns to the dust from whence he came. Here the deceased becomes part of the recollection of those he leaves behind and he is part of their continuing education regarding truth. For example, this is the wisdom of recollection when the parent sees his own death in the life of his children and grandchildren. This is not merely restricted to legacy and continuity. It is also a recognition that he will become death in the lives of these others. This is perhaps the final gift he can give to his loved ones, to teach them one last time of the wisdom gained as death approaches.[6] In these senses, life is in death just as death is in life. But of course the question that remains is whether the deceased will be able to recollect his own death for himself, or perhaps, instead of recollection, there will be bliss and tranquillity that will have no division between mind and God.

As we saw above at the beginning of Chapter 2, the *Phenomenology* ends with the same issue. Absolute spirit has recollection as its new shape. All that it has been lost is also preserved in what is. 'Their preservation [combining] history . . . and the Science of Knowing . . . form alike the inwardizing and the Calvary of Absolute Spirit (Hegel, 1977: 492–93, 1949: 563–64), that is, both life and death. Death has been pivotal to the spiritual education of the reflective subject in this chapter for it has been the formation of every recollection of loss. This was also true, as we saw above, of the relation of self and other. Every educational movement is a death, a loss, a negation. It is how this death is understood that gives what is learned its own shape and content. Spiritual education is what happens when nothing happens. Absolute spirit is absolute because it comes to know death as self-determination, that is, death is the true movement of absolute spirit, and absolute spirit is the truth of death as life. Truth is the experience of death known as formative, as spirit.

Put like this, the question regarding life after death becomes an education that re-forms itself, that is, that re-forms the question. The truth of death is already present. It is what life is. Life is that which knows itself because it has death as other. But the other here is already determinate of life. Therefore the question, 'is there life after death?' is re-formed according to its own actuality. Life is already of death. Life recollects death. Life is already after death. Life must admit its complicity in the positing that underpins the question.

But – and here we raise an issue not taken up in our study of education in Hegel[7] – recollection of death is as much recollection forwards as it is backwards. When death is present as life it is so in the sense that life is both before and after death. Life is after death in that life is victorious in the life and death struggle as the Hegelian spiritual child. Life is also before death as it approaches it in Hegelian old age. Thus life recollects itself in death both backwards and forwards. This groundless standpoint is learning, or is I-philosophy. It is the actuality of time past and time future; the actuality of all time, of eternity known in recollection. This changes how we understand the question as to whether there is life after death. It educates us not to think of their separation on earth and the need for their unification beyond earth. Rather, it educates us to think of life as after death and before death. It commends us, in short, to know the question of life after death as a philosophical education that knows not just their separation but also their actuality, their relationship.

The actuality of this relationship is the recollection of absolute spirit, a relation of truth to itself sustained, lost, and sustained again in learning of the finite in the infinite and the infinite in the finite. As a self-relation absolute spirit is I-philosophy, other than itself and itself as not the other. It is the truth of groundlessness and of death in the life of the individual. It is substance as subject. It is the development, culture and *Aufhebung* of the eternal that is I. It is consciousness, self-consciousness and recollection. This is no longer picture-thinking, this is philosophical education where truth can be known in and by itself. Equally, this is not the reconciliation in any abstract sense of God and the old man. It is only reconciliation in an educational sense, where the reconciliation of subject and substance is in our experience of their difference and not in the overcoming of their difference.

Education in Hegel is not first to comprehend the truth of life as the self-othering of God. But it is perhaps first in comprehending this as a totality of actuality in recollection. The old man faces death, then, from the point of view of its truth, from life. He has recollected his life in the truth of death. His wisdom tells him that he has participated in the life of eternity and has been part of the whole that eternity is. Now he may recollect his death in the truth of life. He knows, also, that wisdom is never closer to its truth than when life and death too are close to each other.

Notes

[1] From *De Principiis Naturae.*

[2] I will not in this chapter explore spiritual education beyond the *Phenomenology*, although previous chapters have attempted this in different ways.

[3] As my Gran said to me, many times.

[4] From Nietzsche, (1982: 522).

[5] The otherness of woman to man and man to woman, as of woman to woman and man to man, will also have its truth in life and death, that is, where I am already other and the other is not me.

[6] Barren educational midwives – teachers – who have no children of their own can find this education in the eternal loss of their pupils. This 'death' of the teacher for the pupil is in the educational truth expressed by Nietzsche that 'one repays a teacher badly if one always remains nothing but a pupil' (1982: 190).

[7] See footnote 11, Introduction.

Bibliography

Adorno, T. W. (1973), *The Jargon of Authenticity*, Evanston: Northwestern University Press.

Adorno, T. W. (1991), 'Why philosophy?' in D. Ingram and J. Simon-Ingram (eds.), *Critical Theory, the Essential Readings*, New York: Paragon House.

Adorno, T. W. (1991), *The Culture Industry*, ed. J. Bernstein, London: Routledge.

Adorno, T. W. (1999), Walter Benjamin and Theodor W. Adorno, *The Complete Correspondence 1928–1940,* ed. H. Lonitz, trans. N. Walker, Cambridge: Polity Press.

Adorno, T. W and Horkheimer, M. (1979), *Dialectic of Enlightenment,* London: Verso.

Al-Ghazali, (1980), *Deliverance from Error,* Louisville: Fons Vitae.

Aquinas, T. (1920), *The 'Summa Theologica' of St. Thomas Aquinas,* Vol. 9, trans. by the Fathers of the English Dominican Province, London: Burns Oates and Washbourne Ltd.

Aquinas, T. (1975a), *Summa Contra Gentiles Book 3,* Part II, Indiana: University of Notre Dame Press.

Aquinas, T. (1975b), *Summa Contra Gentiles Book 4,* Indiana: University of Notre Dame Press.

Aquinas, T. (1998), *Thomas Aquinas: Selected Writings,* London: Penguin Books.

Aristotle, (1984), *The Complete Works of Aristotle (Two Volumes),* ed. J. Barnes, Princeton: Princeton University Press.

Avicenna, (2005), *Metaphysics of the 'The Healing',* trans. M. Marmura, Utah: Brigham University Press.

Beardsworth, R. (1996), *Derrida and the Political,* London: Routledge.

Beardsworth, R. (2006), 'A Note to political understanding of love in our global age', *Contretemps,* available at: http://www.usyd.edu.au/contretemps/contents.html.

Beardsworth, R. (2007), 'Responding to a Post-Script: Philosophy and its Futures', unpublished paper.

Benjamin, W. (1985), *The Origin of German Tragic Drama,* London: Verso.

Benjamin, W. (1992), *Illuminations,* London: Fontana.

Caygill, H. (1998), *Walter Benjamin The Colour of Experience,* London: Routledge.

Caygill, H. (2002), *Levinas and the Political,* London: Routledge.

Cohen, J. (2005), *How to Read Freud,* London: Granta Books.

Derrida, J. (1978), *Writing and Difference,* London: Routledge.

Derrida, J. (1986), *Glas,* Lincoln and London: University of Nebraska Press.

Derrida, J. (1987), *Of Spirit,* Chicago: University of Chicago Press.

Derrida, J. (1988), *Limited Inc,* Evanston: Northwestern University Press.

Derrida, J. (1995), *Points… Interviews 1974–1994,* California: Stanford University Press.

Derrida, J, (2005), *Rogues*, California: Stanford University Press.

Ecclesiasticus, (1916), *The Wisdom of Ben Sira*, London: SPCK, reprinted Kessinger, 2004.

Eliot, T. S. (1944), *Four Quartets*, London: Faber and Faber.

Gallagher, S. (ed.) (1997), *Hegel, History, and Interpretation*, Albany: State University of New York Press.

Hawthorne, N. (1987), *Nathaniel Hawthorne's Tales*, ed. James McIntosh, New York: W. W. Norton and Co.

Harris, H.S. (1995), *Hegel: Phenomenology and System*, Indianapolis: Hackett Publishing Company.

Hegel, G. W. F. (1956), *The Philosophy of History*, trans. J. Sibree, New York: Dover Publications (Werke 12 Vorlesungen über die Philosophie der Geschichte, Frankfurt, Suhrkamp Verlag, 1970).

Hegel, G. W. F. (1967), *Philosophy of Right*, trans. T. M. Knox, Oxford: Oxford University Press.

Hegel, G. W. F. (1969), *Science of Logic*, trans. A. V. Miller, London: George Allen and Unwin.

Hegel, G. W. F. (1974) *Hegel's Lectures on the History of Philosophy Vol. 2*, trans. E. S. Haldane and F. H. Simson, London: RKP; (Werke 19, Vorlesungen über die Geschichte der Philosophie II, Frankfurt, Suhrkamp Verlag, 1970).

Hegel, G. W. F. (1975), *Hegel's Logic: Part One of the Encyclopaedia of the Philosophical Sciences*, trans. W. Wallace, Oxford: Oxford University Press.

Hegel, G. W. F. (1977), *Phenomenology of Spirit*, trans. A. V. Miller, Oxford: Oxford University Press; (Sämtliche Werke; Bd. II, Phänomenologie des Geistes, Leipzig, Meiner, 1949).

Hegel, G. W. F. (1984), *Lectures on the Philosophy of Religion*, Vol. 1, ed. Peter Hodgson, Berkeley: University of California Press.

Hegel, G. W. F. (1986), *The Philosophical Propaedeutic*, trans. A. V. Miller, eds. M. George and A. Vincent, Oxford: Blackwell, (Werke 4 Nürnberger und Heidelberger Schriften 1808–1817, Frankfurt, Suhrkamp Verlag, 1970).

Hegel, G. W. F. (1987), *Introduction to the Lectures on the History of Philosophy*, trans. T. M. Knox and A. V. Miller, Oxford: Clarendon Press, (Sämtliche Werke, Vol. 15a: Vorlesungen über die Geschichte der Philosophie. Einleitung: System und Geschichte der Philosophie. Vollstandig neu nach den Quellen hrsg. V. Johannes Hoffmeister, Leipzig, 1940).

Hegel, G. W. F. (1988), *Lectures on the Philosophy of Religion*; one volume edition, ed. P. Hodgson, Berkeley: University of California Press.

Hegel, G. W. F. (1990), *Hegel's Philosophy of Mind: Part Three of the Encyclopaedia of the Philosophical Sciences*, trans. W. Wallace, Oxford: Oxford University Press.

Heidegger, M. (1987), *An Introduction to Metaphysics*, New Haven: Yale University Press.

Heidegger, M. (1992), *Being and Time*, Oxford: Blackwell.

Kain, P. J. (2005), *Hegel and the Other: A Study of the Phenomenology of Spirit*, New York: State University of New York Press.

Kierkegaard, S. (1983), *Fear and Trembling/Repetition*, trans. H. V. and E. H. Hong, New Jersey: Princeton University Press.

Levinas, E. (1969), *Totality and Infinity*, Pittsburgh: Duquesne University Press; (Totalité et Infini, essai sur l'extériorité, La Haye: Martin Nijhoff, 1961).

Levinas, E. (1998), *Otherwise than Being*, Pittsburgh: Duquesne University Press.

Levinas, E. (2001), *Existence and Existents*, Pittsburgh: Duquesne University Press.

Marcus, L. and Nead, L. (eds.) (1998), *The Actuality of Walter Benjamin*, London: Lawrence and Wishart.

McLaren, P. (1997), *Revolutionary Multiculturalism: Pedagogies of Dissent for the New Millennium*, Oxford: Westview Press.

Nietzsche, F. (1982), *The Portable Nietzsche*, trans. W. Kaufmann, Harmondsworth: Penguin.

Ott, H. (1994), *Martin Heidegger: A Political Life*, London: Fontana Press.

Pascal, B. (1966), *Pensées*, Harmondsworth: London.

Plato, (1956), *Meno*, Harmondsworth: Penguin Books.

Rose, G. (1981), *Hegel Contra Sociology*, London: Athlone.

Rose, G. (1984), *Dialectic of Nihilism*, Oxford: Blackwell.

Rose, G. (1992), *The Broken Middle*, Oxford: Blackwell.

Rose, G. (1993), *Judaism and Modernity*, Oxford: Blackwell.

Rose, G. (1996), *Mourning Becomes the Law*, Cambridge: Cambridge University Press.

Rousseau, J. J. (1973), *The Social Contract and Discourses*, London: Everyman.

Rousseau, J. J. (1974), *Emile*, London: Everyman.

St Augustine, (1972), *City of God*, Harmondsworth: Penguin.

St Augustine, (1998), *Confessions*, Oxford: Oxford University Press.

Swift, J. (1886), *The Battle of the Books and Other Short Pieces*, Forlag: Dodo Press.

Tubbs, N. (2000), 'Mind The Gap; The Philosophy of Gillian Rose', *Thesis Eleven*, 60, Feb, 42–60.

Tubbs, N. (2004), *Philosophy's Higher Education*, Dordrecht: Kluwer.

Tubbs, N. (2005a) 'Fossil fuel culture', *Parallax*, 11, 104–15.

Tubbs, N. (2005b), *Philosophy of the Teacher*, Oxford: Blackwell.

Verene, D. P. (1985), *Hegel's Recollection: a Study of Images in the Phenomenology of Spirit*, Albany: SUNY Press.

Wood, D. (1993), *Of Derrida, Heidegger, and Spirit*, Evanston: Northwestern University Press.

Wood, D. (2002), *Thinking After Heidegger*, Cambridge: Polity Press.

Wordsworth, W. (1965), 'Intimations of immortality from recollections of early childhood,' in Wordsworth's Poems volume 1, London: Dent, 240–46.

Index

Printed in Great Britain
by Amazon.co.uk, Ltd.,
Marston Gate.